Psychology and Sport

Sally Gadsdon

Heinemann

Heinemann Educational Publishers
Halley Court, Jordon Hill, Oxford, OX2 8EJ
a division of Reed Educational & Professional Publishing Ltd

OXFORD MELBOURNE AUCKLAND
JOHANNESBURG BLANTYRE GABORONE
IBADAN PORTSMOUTH NH(USA) CHICAGO

Heinemann is a registered trademark of Reed Educational and Professional Publishing Ltd

05 04 03 02 01
10 9 8 7 6 5 4 3 2 1

British Library Cataloguing in Publication Data
A catalogue record for this book is available from the British Library

ISBN 0 435 80658 0

Typeset by Wyvern 21 Ltd
Picture research by Peter Morris
Printed and bound in Great Britain by The Bath Press Ltd, Bath

Acknowledgements
The publishers would like to thank the following for permission to reproduce copyright material: *The Guardian* for articles on pages 19 and 37; *The Independent*/Syndication for articles on pages 5, 20, 30 and 52; *The Mail* for articles on pages 8–9 and 11.

The publishers would like to thank the following for permission to use photographs: Alan Edwards, page 11; Allsport, pages 25 and 35; Popperfoto, pages 3, 8, 19, 20, 30, 34, 37, 44, 51, 54, 56, 57, 59, and 61.

Cover photograph by AKG London

The publishers have made every effort to contact copyright holders. However, if any material has been incorrectly acknowledged, the publishers would be pleased to correct this at the earliest opportunity

Tel: 01865 888058 www.heinemann.co.uk

Psychology and Sport

Sally Gadsdon

C Contents

Psychology and sport

I) **Introduction**

The application of psychology to the field of sporting performance is relatively new. However, it is possible to apply many traditional psychological concepts and theories to sport and examine new ideas in an attempt to explain the often complex behaviour of sports players. This book is divided into four chapters, each considering a different type of influence upon sporting behaviour – individual differences, psychobiological influences, cognitive influences and social influences.

Chapter 1

The first chapter considers how individual differences affect the way in which sporting situations may be approached. Three main areas are considered: personality theories, learning theories and how sport is taught. Thus the aim is to examine whether the factors and experiences that make an individual unique may link into levels of success in sporting situations.

Chapter 2

The way in which biological influences may affect an individual's sporting behaviour is considered in this chapter: from what motivates an individual to take part in sport in the first place to what makes some players more successful than others, considering the effects of arousal, anxiety and competitiveness.

Chapter 3

This chapter focuses on how an individual's mental processes can affect his/her sporting performance. The different cognitive strategies that sports players may use are considered, with particular focus on the use of imagery, attentional style and the attributions that are made about performance.

Chapter 4

The final chapter considers some of the many social influences on an individual's sporting behaviour. The chapter begins by looking at how children might be socialized into sport, and then considers the effects that others may have on sporting performance, particularly looking at aggression and quality of performance. The chapter also examines how teams function and the importance of leaders on overall performance.

How to use this book

This book has a number of features to help you understand the topic more easily. It is written to give you a wide range of skills in preparation for any of the new AS and A level psychology syllabi. Below is a list of the features with a brief summary to explain how to use them.

1 Real Life Applications

These consist of 'text boxes' which develop further a concept already discussed within the main text. Often they provide articles or outlines of study. In all cases they attempt to apply the theory to real life situations.

2 Commentary

These paragraphs appear throughout the book. They follow on from issues raised within the main text. They serve a number of functions: to provide an evaluation of the earlier text, to clarify a point or to highlight some related issue. Sometimes they provide 'for' and 'against' debates.

3 Key Studies

As the title implies, these are descriptions of important studies within a specific area. There are two of these for each chapter. They briefly identify the aims, method, results and conclusions of the study. This feature helps you to understand the methodology of research.

4 Questions

Each 'Real Life Application' has two or three short answer questions, designed to test a range of skills including: summarizing, outlining and evaluating. All of these activities are designed to allow you to acquire the study skills outlined within the syllabi. In addition, two or three 'essay style' questions are included at the end of each chapter. They relate specifically to the material covered within that chapter.

5 Advice on answering questions

At the end of the book there is a short section that gives brief advice on answering all the essay and short answer questions presented in this book.

1 Individual differences

This chapter examines how individual differences can affect the way sporting situations are approached. Three main themes are considered: personality, learning theories and teaching sport. Through these, the factors that make individuals unique, and the question of whether there is a set of characteristics that enable an individual to be successful in learning and playing sport will be addressed. Real Life Applications that are considered are:

- RLA 1: Family values
- RLA 2: The world's best all-round female athlete
- RLA 3: Karate Sam
- RLA 4: Superstition
- RLA 5: Red card for life
- RLA 6: Conducting a coaching session.

The purpose of discussing personality in connection with psychology and sport is in an attempt to investigate whether certain people are more likely to participate or be successful in sport due their personality characteristics. Personality has formed a large part of sports psychology research.

What is personality?

The concept of personality is difficult to define, as many definitions are seen as too broad or too narrow. One straightforward definition that offers a simple explanation was put forward by Hollander (1971). He described personality as 'the sum total of an individual's characteristics that make him unique'. The important point is that an individual's personality is unique.

Theories of personality

There are a number of different theories that try to explain how personality develops and some of the main ones will be discussed here:

- biological theory
- psychodynamic theory
- humanistic theory
- social learning theory
- trait theory.

Biological theory

Early theories of personality tended to focus upon biological aspects. These have now moved on from the simple ones proposed by the Greeks, which assigned individuals to one of four categories, depending upon the predominance of bodily fluids. However, it is important to note that those who support biological explanations do not believe that all behaviour, all of the time, is under biological influences. There are certain biological factors that influence sporting behaviour – for example, height and body shape – but no sport psychologist would claim that these are the basis of personality, rather that there is an interaction between the biological factors and personality.

Psychodynamic theory

Freud is the most famous psychologist associated with psychodynamic theory. Freud, using self-analysis and detailed observation of patients who were neurotic, carried out much of the early work. His theories have been modified over time. According to Freud, there are three parts to an individual's personality: the id, the ego and the superego. The id is the pleasure-seeking part of personality and is an unconscious, instinctive motive. The ego is the realistic, logical part of personality and the superego is the moral aspect of personality. There are conflicts between the id and the superego, and the ego's role is to assist in resolving these.

According to Freud, aggressive and sexual instincts are major determinants of our personality and thus this links in with aggression in sport (see Chapter 4).

Humanistic theory

The main psychologists associated with this theory are Maslow and Rogers. They believed that individuals possess an inner drive to succeed and better themselves and thus see human nature as healthy and constructive. This contrasts with Freud's rather pessimistic view of humans. The critical concept in connection with this theory is self-actualization. This is the ongoing process whereby individuals seek to achieve their full potential. Maslow developed a hierarchy of needs, which has self-actualization at the pinnacle, but before it can be reached, lower order needs have to be met. Rogers' theory is based around the therapy he used to treat individuals, and he believed that in order for our personality to develop fully we need to be accepted, have unconditional positive regard and not have others' values imposed upon us.

Commentary

Whilst both the psychodynamic and humanistic theories are able to offer an explanation as to how personality develops, both focus on the detailed investigation of individuals. Neither theory has played a significant role in the link between personality and sport.

Trait theory

The main belief of this theory is that individuals possess certain personality traits that are relatively stable and enduring over time. Thus it means that if traits can be identified, behaviour can, to a point, be predicted. A predisposition toward a certain trait does not mean that individuals will always act in that way but that there will be a strong likelihood. For example, a person who has a high level of trait competitiveness would be expected to be competitive in a range of different situations.

Multi-trait theories aim to identify the range of traits that are central to personality and thus give an indication of the person as a whole. The assumption of these theories is that we all share the same basic personality structure but we differ in the amount we display particular traits. The main two trait theorists are Eysenck (1947) and Cattell (1965).

Eysenck studied 700 neurotic, battle-fatigued soldiers and used factor analysis to analyse their personality data. From this he proposed that personality could be broken down into two main dimensions: extroversion–introversion and neuroticism–stability. The belief was that most people would fall around the central point of these, suggesting a normal distribution. He later added a third dimension: psychoticism, the majority of people falling at the lower end of this scale. Although Eysenck's theory is a trait approach to personality, he proposed that the individual differences in extroversion and neuroticism were related to the individual's nervous system, and thus biological in origin. For example, extroverts have lower levels of cortical arousal and therefore seek stimulation in order to enhance their arousal levels, whilst introverts have too much cortical arousal and thus do not actively seek further arousal. Stable individuals have a nervous system that is fairly slow to respond to stressful situations, whilst neurotic individuals' nervous systems respond quickly and strongly. To measure personality he developed the 'Eysenck Personality Inventory' (EPI).

Cattell's work led to the proposal of a more complex theory of personality. He began by collecting more than 18,000 words that could be used to describe personality, and his aim was to reduce these to a number of 'traits' using factor analysis. The initial analysis revealed fifteen source traits which, when further analysed, led to the emergence of sixteen factors. Twelve of the factors were close to the original source traits, three of these source traits failed to re-emerge and four new ones emerged. Thus these sixteen factors led to the development of Cattell's 16 PF as a tool for measuring personality.

Single-trait theorists are not aiming to investigate the whole of personality; rather they are focusing on one aspect of personality and attempting to explain how that personality trait influences behaviour. These include theories such as Rotter's locus of control and McClelland's need for achievement (see pages 38 and 18 for more detail).

Commentary

Trait theories have generated an enormous amount of personality research and offer an appealing approach to the explanation of personality. However, critics argue that identified traits are quite poor predictors of actual behaviour, as people do not always behave in exactly the same way. Trait theories also fail to take into account individuals' experience and the knowledge they have gained about themselves.

Social learning theory

According to social learning theory, behaviour is not

a result of unconscious motives; rather it is learnt through the environment. Thus personality traits are less important as the environment is salient. The main ways in which our personalities develop, according to this theory, are modelling, learning though observation, and through reinforcement (behaviours that are reinforced are likely to be repeated).

Interactionist approach

The preferred approach of many sports psychologists nowadays is the interactionist approach. This considers the relationship between personality factors and situational factors when trying to explain behaviour (see Key Study 1). It does not make simple predictions but does suggest that certain personality factors do influence behaviour and it is important to identify them.

We can see that the relationship between personality and sporting performance is not simple to explain and an individual's sporting ability may have developed in a number of ways. It is well known that there are many families who have more than one member who excels at sport (see RLA 1) and the different theorists would explain this occurrence in different ways.

KEY STUDY 1

Researcher: Moos (1969)

Aim: To investigate the extent of the influence of personality, the situation and the interaction between them.

Method: Psychiatric patients were observed in a number of different situations (for example, on the ward or interacting with therapists) and their behaviour was noted.

Results: Findings were that situational factors accounted for 10% of the observed differences in behaviour, 12% were accounted for by personal characteristics and 21% of differences were due to an interaction between the person and the situation.

Conclusions: The interaction was seen to influence the behaviour more than either the personal characteristics or the situation alone. Therefore in connection with the notion of a 'sporting' personality, it might be more likely that the interaction between personality and the sporting situation is more important.

Real Life Application 1:

Family values

There are surprising numbers of sports players who have another family member who has also excelled at the same sport. Some examples are given below:

Father–son sportsmen

Harry Redknapp – Jamie Redknapp (football)
Graham Hill – Damon Hill (Formula 1)
Brian Clough – Nigel Clough (football)
Frank Lampard – Frank Lampard jnr (football)
Jimmy McRae – Colin McRae (rally driving)

Sibling sports players

Phil and Gary Neville (football)
Martin and Graham Bell (skiing)
Gavin and Scott Hastings (rugby union)
Henry and Robbie Paul (rugby league)
Venus and Serena Williams (tennis)

The Williams sisters

Summary

- From the examples above, it is possible to see that across a range of sports there are members of the same family who are successful at the same sport. There are a number of possible explanations for this.

Questions

1 Why might sporting family relationships raise the nature–nurture debate?

2 How would a trait theorist explain the fact that close family members excel at the same sport?

3 How would a social learning theorist explain this?

Measurement of personality

As there are a number of explanations for personality, there are also a number of different ways to measure it. Many of the techniques are closely linked to a particular theory and it is important to remember that there is no single 'best' test.

There are two main groups of personality test:

- projective tests
- objective tests.

Projective tests are usually used to try to predict some underlying motive for behaviour and link most closely to the psychodynamic theories of personality. The idea is that by using an unstructured test for which there are no right and wrong answers, the individual taking the test is likely to be honest in his/her answers. The best known of these types of tests are the Rorschach Inkblot Test and the Thematic Apperception Test (TAT). The inkblot test was first used in 1921 and remains one of the most popular projective tests. Individuals are presented with 10 cards, one at a time, with symmetrical inkblots on them and have to say what they see, which the tester notes down. The aim is to be able to identify themes or underlying motives in the individual's personality. The inkblot test has not been extensively used in sports psychology as its validity and test–retest reliability has been questioned. The TAT consists of sheets of pictures around which the individual has to make up a story to explain what is happening. Again, this has not been widely used in sports psychology, although the reliability and validity are dependent upon the skill of the person administering it.

Objective measures of personality have been more widely used in sport psychology. They include structured questions, often multiple choice, yes/no or true/false, which are easy to administer and to score. One test that has been used in sports psychology research is the Minnesota Multiphasic Personality Inventory (MMPI), which has more than 500 items measuring a number of different aspects of personality. Eysenck's EPI is a self-report questionnaire that requires yes/no answers and contains a lie scale. It measures personality on the two main dimensions of personality that he proposed. Cattell's 16 Personality Factor questionnaire has also been used and, as the name suggests, the 187 questions measure 16 different opposing personality traits, for example, relaxed–tense.

There are also a number of objective measures that are more relevant to sport but that only measure a limited number of personality characteristics. For example, the Trait Anxiety Inventory (TAI, Spielberger, 1966), the Sport Competition Anxiety Test (SCAT, Martens, 1977) and the Test of Attentional and Interpersonal Style (TAIS, Nideffer, 1976). Further discussion of these specific tests can be found in Chapter 2.

Commentary

It is questionable whether the structured objective tests for personality are an adequate method of measuring human personality. Is it possible to reduce personality to a series of yes/no answers, as in the EPI?

Sport and personality research
Credulous–sceptical argument

Some psychologists believe that personality tests are very useful tools as predictors of sports behaviour, whilst others believe them to be useless. Morgan (1979) presented this argument as the credulous–sceptical argument. He noted that psychologists seemed to belong to one of two groups regarding the usefulness of personality traits to predict athletic success. Firstly there was the credulous group who believed that personality profiles could be useful, and secondly there was the sceptical group who believed that such profiles had little or no use. Morgan suggested that neither group was correct and he believed that athletic success was partly due to personality traits, but that situation was also important (Morgan was therefore adopting an interactionist viewpoint).

Athletes and non-athletes

A great deal of research has been carried out over a prolonged period of time in an attempt to identify the characteristics of a sporting personality. Some of the earliest work was by Griffith in the 1920s and he found that great athletes tended to have, amongst others, the following characteristics: 'courage, intelligence, optimism, alertness, conscientiousness'. Research since this has found very similar results, even when more sport-specific measures were introduced.

Some more recent research was carried out by Morgan (1980), and following a series of studies he proposed the 'mental health model' which suggests that mental health and success in sport are directly related. Having studied athletes from a range of different sports, including wrestlers and distance runners, and athletes of different skill levels, he found that successful athletes had more positive mental health characteristics than the general population. This had been measured using the Profile of Mood States (POMS) and Morgan termed the profile of the successful athlete that emerged as the 'iceberg profile'.

Commentary

Although Morgan's model is based on extensive research, it must be noted that the model is quite general and not all athletes have the suggested profile and some non-athletes do. It is also difficult to identify the direction of causality, and it may be that successful athletes have more positive mental health characteristics because they are successful.

Different sport, different personality type?

As we can see from the information presented above, there are general differences in the personalities of sports players and non-sports players. Other studies have aimed to investigate whether there is simply a 'sporting personality' or whether the personality characteristics of sports players differ from sport to sport. Some of the earliest work in this field was carried out looking at bodybuilders, and research by Harlow (1951) suggested that bodybuilders tend to suffer from feelings of masculine inadequacy. Later research did not support these initial stereotypes.

Kroll and Crenshaw (1970) carried out a study using highly skilled sports players from a range of sports: football, wrestling, gymnastics and karate. They all completed Cattell's 16 PF and the results showed that wrestlers and footballers had similar profiles, whilst the gymnasts and the karate participants differed from each other as well as from the wrestlers and the footballers.

Other differences in personality profiles have been found between players of individual and team sports (Schurr, Ashley and Joy, 1977). Team sports players were more anxious, dependent and extroverted but less sensitive and imaginative than individual sports players.

Commentary

Whilst some research has found there to be differences in the personality profiles of the participants of different sports, it must be treated with caution as other research has not substantiated the early findings. Therefore, whilst they may provide a useful insight into the participants of different sports, personality profiles should not be used on their own to categorize players.

The élite athlete

Research has found that élite athletes do tend to fit Morgan's 'iceberg profile'. A number of studies have investigated the notion of the 'élite' athlete's profile and generally they have found that élite athletes are low in anxiety and neuroticism and high in extroversion. When measuring mood states, élite athletes are low in anxiety, tension, depression, anger, fatigue and confusion but high in vigour. An example of an élite athlete, Denise Lewis, is considered in RLA 2.

Real Life Application 2:
The world's best all-round female athlete

When Denise Lewis won the gold medal for the heptathalon, at the Sydney 2000 Olympics, she became the world's finest all-round female athlete. In order to achieve this accolade Denise Lewis has shown great determination and vigour. When her mother arranged for her to join an athletics group when she was fourteen years old, it took her an hour and a half to get there and an hour and a half to get home. Denise, however, went four nights a week, demonstrating her determination at an early stage. Denise loves sport, she claims that she gets energy, a sort of buzz, from athletics. She also believes that she has the same inner strength as her mother.

When she was nineteen she suffered a serious knee injury that threatened to hamper her athletics career, however she successfully learnt to lead with her weaker left knee to overcome this problem. Despite disappointment at not winning the gold at Atlanta in 1996 or at the Commonwealth Games in 1998, Denise fought back and planned with her coach how she could win the gold at Sydney. Their strategy paid off.

Adapted from 'The bright-eyed girl with a will of steel' by Simon Turnbull, *The Independent*, 25 September 2000.

Summary

• Denise Lewis can be considered to be one of the world's élite athletes. Her route to success has not always been easy, yet she has demonstrated great determination throughout.

Questions

1 Why is Denise Lewis considered to be a world-class élite athlete?

2 Describe how Denise Lewis fits into Morgan's 'iceberg profile' for élite athletes.

Learning

In order to progress in sport, young players must learn and master new skills. It is therefore essential that to ensure learning takes place, teachers and coaches have an understanding of learning theory. Learning is defined as any relatively permanent change in behaviour due to experience, and learning theory is based around the belief that behaviour is observable. The work related to learning theory began at the turn of the twentieth century and is what is known as behaviourism.

Learning can be simple or complex and there are three main ways in which we learn:

• we make associations
• we repeat actions
• we watch and copy others.

Three theories of learning will be considered in this section, linked to the above:

• classical conditioning
• operant conditioning
• social learning theory.

Classical conditioning

The initial work in this field was carried out by Russian physiologist, Ivan Pavlov. Pavlov was researching the digestive systems of dogs and by accident discovered that the dogs were salivating prior to the presentation of food, simply at the sight of the research assistant who normally brought their food. Following further investigations to explain this, the psychological phenomena of classical conditioning was developed. Classical conditioning is a form of learning that involves involuntary, reflex responses. The learning process starts with an unconditioned stimulus (UCS): in the dogs' case, the food, which leads to an unconditioned response (UCR), salivation. A neutral stimulus can become the conditioned stimulus (CS) if presented simultaneously or just before the unconditioned stimulus. Thus in this case, the conditioned stimulus was the researcher and following repeated pairings with the unconditioned stimulus, the conditioned stimulus alone resulted in salivation, which is known as a conditioned response (CR). Further experiments demonstrated that the dogs could learn to associate anything with food, such as a bell, leading to a conditioned response (see Figure 1.1 for the stages of classical conditioning).

Figure 1.1: The process of classical conditioning

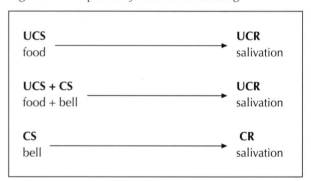

Before considering the application of classical conditioning in a sporting setting, it is important to note some of the other characteristics of classical conditioning. Extinction (i.e. the conditioned response ceases) occurs if the conditioned stimulus is continually presented without the unconditioned stimulus. However, if the unconditioned stimulus is presented again, a spontaneous recovery may occur for the conditioned stimulus. Other features of classical conditioning are generalization and discrimination. Generalization means that the conditioned response occurs when stimuli similar to the conditioned stimulus are presented. For example, the dog may salivate to any bell sound, not just the specific conditioned one. Discrimination is the opposite effect and occurs if the unconditioned stimulus is presented with only one specific conditioned stimulus. Therefore, if the food was only presented at the sound of a particular bell the dog would learn to discriminate between the sounds.

Classical conditioning and sport

RLA 3 demonstrates how classical conditioning can occur in human behaviour linked to sport.

Real Life Application 3:

Karate Sam

Imagine a six-year-old child, Sam, who is shy and does not enjoy being with lots of different people. Sam's parents decide to take him to karate classes to meet other people, in an attempt to help him overcome his shyness. Before each session, Sam feels anxious and does not look forward to it. After a few weeks his parent's buy him the 'suit' to wear to the weekly sessions. Sam puts it on just before setting off for the class. Soon just the sight of the outfit hanging in his wardrobe is sufficient to make him feel anxious as he has learnt to associate it with the anxiety of attending classes.

Summary

• This example illustrates how classical conditioning can work in a real life setting, often without any direct intention for learning to take place.

Questions

1 Make a copy of the box below and fill in the gaps to demonstrate the process of classical conditioning.

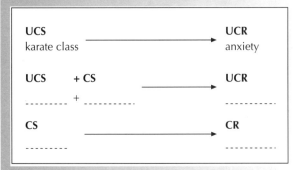

UCS		UCR
karate class	⟶	anxiety
UCS + CS	⟶	UCR
.... + ...		....
CS	⟶	CR
....		....

2 Explain how generalization might occur as a result of Sam's conditioning.

3 How do you think you could use classical conditioning to reverse the effects of the anxiety?

It is also possible to use classical conditioning to positive effect in a sport setting. If an individual is taught to associate a technique with relaxation it can then be used to reduce anxiety. For example, if the sports player is taught to relax and then learn a phrase, such as 'stay calm', in a competitive situation saying 'stay calm' should lead to the individual feeling more relaxed.

Commentary

Whilst it is possible to explain some types of learning via classical conditioning it is important to remember that learning by association in this way works only on reflex responses. As humans have a rather limited number of such responses, we need to look to other types of learning to explain how more complex skills develop.

Operant conditioning

Whilst classical conditioning is concerned with involuntary behaviours, operant conditioning is concerned with all other types of learning. Initial work was carried out by Thorndike, working with cats and later continued by Skinner who worked with rats and pigeons.

Thorndike placed cats into a 'puzzle box' which was basically a cage with the door that could be opened from the inside by pulling a piece of rope. After the cat had been in the box for a period of time it would pull the rope by accident and the door would open. The cat was placed back into the box and the door was again closed. Thorndike timed how long it took for the cat to escape and found that each trial took less time. This was termed trial and error leaning. Thorndike believed that the reward (the freedom) was responsible for 'stamping in' the correct response. From these experiments he developed the principle of the Law of Effect, which states that behaviour that results in pleasant consequences is more likely to be repeated, whereas behaviour that has no pleasant consequences will be less likely to be repeated.

Skinner continued Thorndike's work via laboratory experiments with rats. He placed the rats into a box that contained a lever that, when pressed, would dispense food. As the rats explored their surroundings they would accidentally press the lever and a food pellet would be released. This reward (reinforcement) could then be used to get the rat to respond to different things and thus demonstrate 'behaviour shaping'. Skinner illustrated how behaviour could be shaped by using reinforcers each time the behaviour got close to what he required, and he taught pigeons to play Ping-Pong in this way. Skinner also demonstrated that different schedules of reinforcement could be used; thus a behaviour does not, after the initial learning has taken place, need to be reinforced every time. The features of classical conditioning – extinction, generalization and discrimination – may also occur in operant conditioning and this must not be forgotten when developing the schedule of reinforcement. Therefore, the most important feature of operant conditioning is reinforcement. However, this does not have to be positive. Negative reinforcement (the removal of something unpleasant) and punishment (the delivery of something unpleasant) can be used.

Commentary

Whilst a range of different reinforcers can be used and a variety of schedules, for learning to take place most effectively it is best to use positive reinforcers. Generally, continuous reinforcement (reward is given for every instance of the desired behaviour) produces the quickest learning, whilst partial reinforcement (reward is only given some of the time) produces learning that lasts longer in the absence of rewards.

Positive reinforcement

In the world of sport there is a wide range of different positive reinforcers, including praise and trophies for amateur sports players and extra pay and extensions of contracts for professional sports players. Punishment may also be used in an attempt to modify behaviour, such as verbal reprimands, suspensions and fines.

Operant conditioning can be widely applied in a sport setting. Obviously, the use of reinforcement can be utilized to teach sports participants new skills. Imagine a situation where a coach is trying to develop penalty-taking skills in a youth football team. S/he should use praise to encourage the players and could possibly think about other reinforcers, such as privileges, to attempt to get them to practise their skills further. One of the team's players is apprehensive about taking penalties and as a result avoids joining in the practice sessions. The coach could use operant conditioning to try to improve this situation by shaping the player's behaviour. Initially,

the coach would need to reinforce the player if he was willing to take part in the session, then further reinforcement would need to be given for kicking the ball around near to the goal. This type of reinforcement would need to continue until the player felt confident enough to practise penalty taking.

Operant conditioning may be able to explain superstitious behaviour in the sports world. As the law of effect states that a behaviour that is reinforced is likely to be repeated, in sport, behaviour that leads to winning is likely to be repeated. Thus sports players may develop beliefs that they can only perform well if they are wearing certain articles of clothing or a particular number, due to the fact that they won when wearing that clothing previously and therefore believe that it was an integral part of the result. Another example of such a ritual is Fabien Barthez, the French national goalkeeper, being kissed on the head by Laurent Blanc at the start of national games, which began after the team won when Blanc first did this. It has now become a part of their behaviour, as the positive reinforcement (winning) led to it being repeated. RLA 4 examines further superstitious behaviour in sport.

Real Life Application 4: Superstition

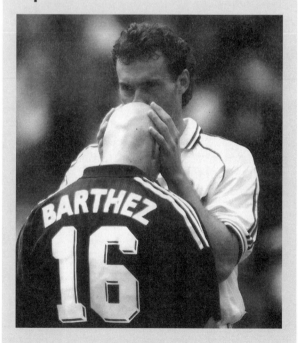

Laurent Blanc kisses Fabien Barthez

Sport may demand physical training, but just as important is mental preparation. Little rituals and superstitions may seem primitive and pointless but for sports players they can help to build self-confidence, banish self-doubt and concentrate the mind.

It appears that superstitious behaviour occurs in sports players from a wide range of different sports. Champion golfer Tiger Woods still wears red on the final day of prestigious tournaments, which he explains goes back to the fact that he is a Capricorn and red is Capricorn's lucky colour. In the world of motor racing, Michael Schumacher will always get into his car from the left-hand side and David Coulthard takes his 'lucky' pair of underpants (the ones he wore when he won his first Grand Prix in 1995) with him to every race. Alexander Wurz wears a red racing boot on his left foot and a blue one on his right. This ritual dates back to when a team-mate hid his racing boots and he had to put on the first boots that he could find, although they did not match. He won that Formula Ford race and believed that the mis-matching boots were a lucky charm and he has continued to wear them since then. In team games it is often the more solitary figures, such as the goalkeeper, who are most likely to indulge in ritualistic behaviour. For example, Peter Schmeichel, former Manchester United goalkeeper, would hug the goalposts before each game.

Adapted from the *Mail on Sunday*, Night and Day magazine, 10 September 2000.

Summary

- Top sports players may find that carrying out certain rituals before or during sporting events may help them to focus their minds.
- Although it is unlikely that the ritual itself has any effect on their sporting performance, if it allows them to concentrate and mentally prepare for the event more successfully, it could be said to serve a useful purpose.

Questions

1 How may the fact that Alexander Wurz wears different coloured boots be explained by operant conditioning?

2 How can performing superstitious behaviours help sports players' self-confidence?

Negative reinforcement and punishment

Negative reinforcement may also be used in sport. Imagine a girl who does not enjoy PE lessons at school and detests playing hockey. She starts off trying to tackle opponents but is constantly unsuccessful. This in turn leads to her not trying to tackle in the future and as a result the teacher allows her to go and practise her tackling with a friend. Therefore, the unpleasant situation, playing in a game of hockey, has been removed and the girl's behaviour (i.e. not trying) has been reinforced. It is likely that she will adopt the same tactics in the future.

Punishment is also used in sport but, as mentioned above, it may weaken behaviour and is not as effective as reinforcement. Punishment in sport includes yellow and red cards in football, sending players off for bad behaviour or not allowing them to play in future matches.

Social learning theory

Albert Bandura took learning theory a stage further and developed Social Learning Theory. He accepted the basic principles of classical and operant conditioning but believed that conditioning on its own is inadequate to explain the majority of human social behaviour. He also believed that reinforcement was not as vitally important as Skinner believed and thought that it is not possible to explain learning fully without looking at the cognitive processes involved.

Therefore, Bandura put forward an alternative to conditioning – social learning theory – focusing on imitation. He suggested that we can learn by watching a model and copying, which is obviously more effective than trial and error learning (see Figure 1.2). He suggested that a four-step process is required for observational learning. The first two steps involve cognitive processes. Firstly, attention to the behaviour that is to be imitated is required. Secondly, memory is needed to store the observed behaviour, as without a memory of what has been observed it is unlikely to be repeated. The third step is the motor reproduction of the behaviour, putting into practice what has been observed. The final part to Bandura's stages is motivation, as without the motivation to attend to, remember and reproduce the behaviour, learning is unlikely to occur.

Commentary

In order to make learning most effective it is important for the coach to highlight the relevant aspects of behav-

Figure 1.2: Bandura's four step model

iour that the individuals should be paying attention to. It would also be beneficial if the coach helped the sports players to develop their mental rehearsal skills in order to assist in remembering exactly how the model performed. The individual should be allowed to practise the observed skill and receive appropriate feedback from the coach to help develop the skill. Coaches can also help to improve players' motivation (see Chapter 2).

Reinforcement

Social learning theory still maintains that reinforcement is important, but it can be direct or vicarious. There are also certain characteristics that affect how likely an individual is to imitate behaviour. Bandura found that children are more likely to imitate people who they perceive to be similar to them in some way. Also, an individual who appears to have some power and control over something desirable will be more likely to be imitated, as will a warm and caring individual.

Self-modelling

A number of researchers, who support the social learning theory viewpoint, are starting to believe in the value of self-modelling. This simply involves individuals viewing themselves carrying out a particular task. Generally this is done by watching a videotape of them performing the task or skill correctly. As it is important that the individuals see themselves performing perfectly, some editing of the video may be required by the coach. The idea is that by watching themselves performing successfully their skills will be further enhanced as they model their behaviour on the perfect example. Key Study 2 examines how this may work in a sports setting.

Social learning theory and sport

Coaches should be able to use the principles of social learning theory to improve players' learning of certain skills. It may be appropriate for the coach to demonstrate skills for the player to model or, alternatively, to allow the players to observe their sporting heroes perform skills and thus act as 'models'. Examples can be seen throughout sport – for example, the Michael Owen soccer school, which

---

KEY STUDY 2

Researchers: Templin and Vernacchia (1995)

Aim: To investigate the usefulness of self-modelling in sport.

Method: Five male college basketball players took part in the study. The researchers videotaped the players during home games. The videos were edited to provide an individual self-modelling tape for each player. Inspirational music was added to the tapes, chosen by each individual. The final video lasted for between three and five minutes. The players were asked to view the tapes prior to predetermined games during the season. The researchers compared the players' shooting accuracy before and after watching the self-modelling videotape.

Results: The results showed that for three out of the five players there was an increase in performance after watching the videos.

Conclusions: Although this is only a small-scale study the findings are interesting. If, following further investigation, these results are common to other sports this self-modelling technique could prove very useful to help sports players practise. The video would assist practice, copying a successful example, in between training sessions, which may lead to mastery of skills in a shorter time.

---

was televised, showed Michael demonstrating particular skills that young players observed and attempted to imitate. The rewards for these players would be feedback from Michael and vicariously feeling that they are like Michael Owen, who is rich and famous.

Young sports players are more likely to imitate a

behaviour if they see the 'model' as successful and it is therefore important for élite performers to behave well. If youngsters see their sporting heroes behaving badly and still getting rewarded they are likely to copy the bad behaviour (see Chapter 4 for further discussion). The potential effects on individuals copying their sporting heroes' bad behaviour can be seen in RLA 5.

Real Life Application 5:
Red card for life

A fifteen-year-old boy has been banned from football for life after punching a referee. The boy, who played in goal in a junior football league, ran to the half way line at full time to confront the referee about how he handled the game, in which his team had lost. He threw two punches at the referee which both made contact. He was sent off and following a disciplinary hearing has been banned from playing football competitively anywhere in the world. The referee, who was treated for cuts and bruises, blamed the behaviour of Premiership footballers such as Roy Keane for setting young players a bad example. He believes that the young players are watching these players on the TV and following their behaviour.

Adapted from the *Daily Mail*, 18 August 2000.

Summary

- This case illustrates how learning theory may be applied in a real life setting, as by punishing the boy it is putting out a message to other young players that this type of behaviour is unacceptable.

Questions

1 Has the boy in this case received positive reinforcement, negative reinforcement or punishment for his actions?

2 Which theory can explain how the coach believes the boy learnt this behaviour?

3 Explain how children may learn behaviour by watching their 'heroes' play.

The coach's role in assisting learning

Alongside the general ways in which the coach can help young players, there are also some specific forms of guidance that can be given. This leads on to the next area to consider – teaching sport. Although individuals may learn in different ways, successful mastery of a new skill is often dependent upon the effectiveness of the teaching that the player has received (this also links in with leadership, which is discussed in Chapter 4, see page 57).

Forms of guidance

There are a number of ways that a coach may give guidance to players. Three will be considered here:

- verbal
- visual
- manual.

Verbal guidance involves the coach speaking to the players, either giving instructions or feedback, in an effort to improve their skills. This type of guidance may be used alone or in conjunction with the other types of guidance. Verbal guidance needs to be clear, concise and relevant. Coaches may use verbal guidance during practice games to get players to be more aware of keeping their positions.

Visual guidance links in very closely with the social learning theory's proposals about learning. With this type of guidance the coach provides a demonstration of a particular skill for the player to copy. As the whole skill is demonstrated the player is able to remember it and ultimately reproduce it. The coach may use this technique if, for example, s/he wanted the players to learn a passing technique.

Visual and verbal guidance – a coach demonstrates a new skill

Manual guidance involves the coach providing physical guidance while a skill is being learnt. This gives the individual extra confidence and a sense of security while they become familiar with the new skill. An example of when the coach may use manual guidance could be when a young rugby player is learning how to hold a ball before a kick. The coach may put his/her hands over the player's to help the player get a 'feel' for how it should be done.

Commentary

It can be seen that there are a number of different ways that a coach can provide guidance to a player. However, it must be remembered that no one type of guidance will be suitable for all players or all situations. The skill of the coach is therefore being able to recognize when to adopt the different types of guidance.

Teaching styles

The way that information is presented to learners can affect how successful their learning is. Again there is not one single 'best' method, rather success depends upon a number of factors. The influence of the teacher varies, depending on what teaching style they are using. Mosston and Ashworth (1986) identified a variety of different teaching styles and put forward a Spectrum of Teaching Styles. At one end of this continuum the teacher makes all the decisions (the command style) whilst at the other end the learner makes most of the decisions (the discovery style). Below are the four styles on this continuum.

Command style

A teacher adopting this style of teaching would be very authoritarian (see Chapter 4 on leadership styles, page 57) and thus would make all the decisions and treat all individuals in virtually the same way. There would be little opportunity for discussion or social contact between learners. Although this style would not be appropriate in many situations, as it does not allow the learner much scope to develop individually, it does have its uses. For example, the command style would be suitable for teaching a class of primary school children how to perform a new skill in the gym. It could also be used in situations where the information to be given is the same for all members of the group – for example, a line dancing class or a keep fit class.

Commentary

The command style enables the teacher to exercise a great degree of control over what is taught and it can be very effective for the teaching of new skills as the learners are able to copy what the teacher instructs them to do. The drawback with this style of teaching is that it prevents the learners taking any responsibility for their own learning and thus may reduce their levels of intrinsic motivation. It is also unlikely that there will be much opportunity for the teacher to provide specific feedback to individuals and this again may reduce the motivation of the learners.

Reciprocal style

Moving along the spectrum of teaching styles, reciprocal style allows the learners to be much more involved in their own learning. The teacher still decides what is to be taught but the learners work in pairs and take it in turns to be the performer and the observer. The benefit of working in pairs is that it provides the opportunity for instant feedback, allowing for improvements to be made. The teacher monitors the learning and provides guidance where necessary.

Commentary

This style of teaching obviously overcomes some of the problems with the command style as the learner has a more active role. However, in order for this style to work, it is essential that all of the learners have some basic skills, and it is thus more suitable for developing more complex skills. The instant feedback will help to maintain motivation and improve self-confidence. However, there is a risk that the feedback from the other learner may be inappropriate or incorrect and this could lead to the skills being learnt incorrectly. Although the teacher is not as 'visible', there is a great deal of pressure on teachers using this style, as each pair needs to be carefully monitored.

Problem-solving style

Again, this style allows the learner to have a greater amount of input into their learning and, as with the reciprocal style, it is more suited for teaching more advanced skills. The style involves the teacher setting problems for the learner to solve. This allows the learners to think about their sport and be creative in their solutions. The teacher has limited control over how the learners work. It is most suitable if the learners are required to apply their existing knowledge to a novel situation.

Commentary

The benefits of this style of teaching are that it increases the learners' understanding of the sport and thus will increase their levels of motivation and self-efficacy. It may also provide valuable experience of decision-making and problem-solving for players who have to make their own decisions on the pitch. The success of this style of teaching is dependent upon the learners being confident in expressing their thoughts and solutions to the problems.

Discovery style

This style of teaching requires the teacher to adopt the role of facilitator, allowing the learners to discover things for themselves. There are some similarities between this and the problem-solving style of learning, although problem solving focuses more on specific aspects of skills whilst discovery learning is more open-ended. Thus in this style of teaching, the teacher gives clues and hints to get a player to think about ways of improving particular skills.

Commentary

Again, this approach is most suitable for learners who already have quite well developed skills in their particular sport. It is probably the best way of teaching sports that require a high level of creativity, such as dance. It is, however, necessary to ensure that this style is specific to each individual and therefore it can be very time consuming for the teacher. This aspect is in contrast to the instructive approach of the command style of teaching.

Using the different styles

It can be seen that there are a variety of different ways to teach sport. It is therefore important that the teacher or coach takes into account individual differences and preferences for different styles when attempting to teach new skills (see RLA 6). A good teacher or coach will be able to use the different techniques, as and when appropriate.

Real Life Application 6:

Conducting a coaching session

As it appears that many children are spending longer and longer in front of the TV, it is becoming increasingly challenging for coaches to prevent children dropping out of sport. It is therefore important for coaches to look for alternatives to traditional coaching methods. When children are asked what qualities they would like to see in a coach they invariably say that they want someone who is enthusiastic, energetic, patient, understanding and above all, has a sense of humour. Coaches are being encouraged to take these messages on board when they are planning sessions and are being advised about the style training sessions should take. For example, the suggestion is that sessions should last between 45 and 75 minutes, depending on factors such as players' stamina and ability. It is also important, particularly when the children are new to the sport, not to play any 'elimination' games, as it is those players who need most practice who will be deprived of practice time.

Thus the whole aim of coaching sessions should be to allow the children to have fun and make the experience positive and fulfilling. Coaches should aim to keep the children on task as much as possible, vary activities, provide opportunities for repeated practice and give positive feedback.

Adapted from 'Conducting a coaching session' by Christopher Saffici, *Journal of Physical Education, Recreation and Dance*, October 1998, published by the American Alliance for health, Physical Education, Recreation and Dance, 1900 Assocation Dr., Reston, VA 20191, USA.

Summary

- A coach can have an impact on children's enjoyment of sport. It is important for coaches to be trained before they attempt to train others.

Questions

1 Why do you think that it is important that training sessions for children do not last longer than 75 minutes?

2 Why do you think coaches should allow opportunities for repeated practice within a training session?

3 Apart from missing out on training time, what other effects do you think playing elimination games may have on children?

Successful sports teaching and coaching

During this chapter – which has focused on individual differences linked to personality, learning and teaching sport – a number of points have been raised that are relevant to successful teaching and coaching. Whilst there are many other important points raised in the other chapters, below is a list of key points that are drawn from this chapter:

- Use reinforcement liberally in the early stages of learning, remembering not to focus solely on extrinsic motivators.
- Avoid the use of punishment, particularly in the early stages of learning.
- Provide suitable role models, both for skill learning and general sporting behaviour.
- Allow opportunities for the learners to experience success in an attempt to raise their levels of self-efficacy and increase their likelihood of continuing with the sport.
- Emphasize the mastery of skills rather than the competitive element of the sport, particularly for young children.
- Attempt to develop appropriate associations, reversing any negative associations with sport that may already be present.
- Allow the learners to have some input into their learning to maintain their motivation.
- Provide instructions in a clear, concise manner, allowing an opportunity to practise as soon as possible.

Essay questions

1 Describe and evaluate one main theory of personality and how it explains why some people take part in sport and other people do not.

2 A teacher wants a small group of six-year-olds to learn how to perform a forward roll in gymnastics. Explain how both operant conditioning and social learning theory could be used to enable the children to learn.

3 Describe the style of teaching that you believe would be the best way to teach intermediate level footballers new ball skills. Justify your choice.

2 Psychobiology and sport

This chapter considers some biological influences upon our behaviour that can affect whether we take part in sport in the first place and what might make some sports players more successful than others. Four main topics will be considered: motivation, arousal, competitiveness and anxiety. Real Life Applications that are considered are:

- RLA 7: Picking teams
- RLA 8: Sydney's female form
- RLA 9: McRae's motivation
- RLA 10: Jarrett clatters to gold.

Motivation

Motivation is an important topic to consider when trying to explain why some people take part in sports and others appear very reluctant to join in. The main question that needs to be answered is: what motivates someone to take part in a sporting activity?

It is necessary first to consider what exactly is meant by the term motivation. One definition of motivation is that it is 'the internal mechanisms and external stimuli which arouse and direct behaviour' (Sage, 1974). There are three points that arise from this definition. Firstly, it suggests that motivation involves inner drives; secondly it also suggests that motivation involves external forces and finally, due to the first two combining, it thus suggests that motivation leads to the intensity and direction of our behaviour.

It is generally accepted that there are two main sources of motivation:

- intrinsic
- extrinsic.

Intrinsic motivation is motivation that comes from within a person whilst extrinsic motivation is motivation that comes from the surrounding environment. If we consider sport players it will usually be a combination of internal factors (such as wanting to participate and do well) and external factors (for example, praise and rewards) that motivates them to take part in their sport. It is often difficult to try to separate motivating factors completely, as frequently external factors may feed into inner drives, and vice versa.

Intrinsic motivation

Duda (1989) identified three motivational factors that could be considered to be intrinsic motivators. These are:

- to have mastery over a task
- to display superiority
- to gain social approval.

One theory that has been put forward to explain what affects our intrinsic motivation, and how this in turn can affect performance and link with extrinsic motivators, is the Cognitive Evaluation Theory (Deci and Ryan, 1985). This theory proposes that individuals have an innate (in-built) need to feel personally competent and self-determining. However, self-determination can be seen as either internally or externally caused, and depending upon an individual's perception of it, their intrinsic motivation increases or decreases.

Intrinsic motivation will be at its highest when an individual feels competent and self-determining in a given situation. Sport settings can provide opportunities for individuals to compare their skills and personal competencies against a standard. According to the Cognitive Evaluation Theory, there are two aspects to the feedback that an individual receives:

- controlling
- informational.

The controlling aspect links to an individual's locus of causality and if s/he perceives the setting to be controlling. For example, the pressure on the striker in the school football team, from the coach, to score to win for the glory of the school. This will lead to an external locus of causality and thus a low level of self-determination, and ultimately a decline in intrinsic motivation. An event where the controlling aspect is seen internally – for example, an individual's input into their personal training programme – will lead to increases in intrinsic motivation.

The informational aspect of the feedback provides information to the individual about their personal competence. Thus positive information, such as an athlete discovering their 100-metre time was a personal best, will lead to feelings of personal competence and thus lead to increases in intrinsic motivation. On the other hand, negative information, such as criticism from the coach, will lead to lower levels of personal competence and consequently lower levels of intrinsic motivation.

The effect that the controlling and informational aspects of feedback have on an individual's intrinsic motivation will be dependent upon which one s/he perceives as most salient.

Commentary

According to Cognitive Evaluation Theory élite performers have a strong need to demonstrate their personal competence and self-determination, thus they commit themselves to difficult and demanding goals, and achieving these further enhances their intrinsic motivation. If an élite performer does not achieve these demanding goals this theory would suggest that this would lead to a reduction in perceived personal competence, and ultimately a reduction in intrinsic motivation. However, this reduction does not always occur, as often failure to reach set goals leads to greater self-determination within the individual to achieve the goals in future attempts. It would also be important for the performers to receive positive feedback, or at the very least constructive feedback, to ensure that they feel rewarded and thus maintain their intrinsic motivation. This theory would also suggest that it is important for sports players to feel that they are responsible, to some extent, for their training and performance to maintain their levels of intrinsic motivation. Both of these final two factors could have important implications for coaches (see 'The coach's role in assisting learning' in Chapter 1, page 11).

Studies have been carried out to look at the effect of feedback on intrinsic motivation, thus looking at the salience of the informational aspect (see Key Study 3).

KEY STUDY 3

Researchers: Vallerand and Reid (1984)

Aim: To assess the effect of feedback on performance.

Method: 115 male adults took part in stage 1 of the study. They were assessed on their intrinsic motivation and perceived competence on a stabilometer task. 84 participants who had at least moderate levels of intrinsic motivation were asked to continue to the second stage. The participants were randomly assigned to one of three conditions (positive feedback, negative feedback and no feedback) on a stabilometer balance task. The task required them to try to maintain their balance throughout the 20-second trials.

Results: Positive feedback condition scored highest on an intrinsic motivation measure (Task Reaction Questionnaire (Mayo, 1977)), then the no feedback condition, with negative feedback condition scoring lowest.

Conclusions: The study highlights how the type of feedback that sports players receive can affect their subsequent performance and, as this study has shown, positive feedback appears to have the best effect on performance.

Intrinsic motivation has really only been measured in relation to feedback and therefore research is needed to look at other aspects.

Extrinsic motivation

An individual's motivation from the surrounding environment, often in the form of rewards, both tangible and intangible, is known as extrinsic motivation. Tangible rewards include badges, medals and prize money, whilst intangible rewards include praise from parents or peers, gaining a record time or title and achieving recognition. The use of external rewards to increase motivation links in with learning theories (see Chapter 1), as the rewards used are acting as reinforcers to increase the likelihood of an action being repeated in the future.

Teachers and coaches must be careful to ensure that external rewards do not overtake the intrinsic motivation. It is important to strike a balance between the two and ensure that the emphasis put on winning is not so great that it detracts from the pleasure of taking part. Research has found that the expectation of a reward for taking part in an event can lead to a reduction in the amount of pleasure derived from simply taking part in the activity.

Primary and secondary motivation

Motivation to take part can be split in a different way into primary and secondary motivation. Primary motivation comes from the positive or negative effects of taking part in the activity itself, whilst secondary motivation comes from the positive or negative effects of any source of influence other than the activity itself. Examples of a primary motivator in sport would include the feelings of achievement when successful – for example, completing a marathon in a personal best time. A secondary motivator in sport could be receiving a bonus for playing well or being appointed as captain of the team.

The motivational sequence

Vallerand and Losier (1999) proposed a motivational sequence that integrates intrinsic and extrinsic motivation (see Figure 2.1)

Figure 2.1 illustrates how the impact of social factors is dependent upon the individual's perception of them. Further research is needed to test this proposal further – however, it does have potentially important implications for teachers and coaches. This sequence demonstrates that there is a relationship between a variety of factors and an individual's motivation. RLA 7 illustrates how the interaction of factors may affect an individual's motivation to participate in sport.

Real Life Application 7:

Picking teams

Imagine that you are a ten-year-old boy, Jamie, taking part in a school PE lesson. The teacher has told the class that the boys are going to be playing football and elects two boys, generally acknowledged as the best footballers in the class, to be captains. You enjoy playing football because you like running around and taking part in a game with your friends and after all, your parents have taught you that winning is not the most important thing. All the boys line up to be 'chosen' for the teams. Each captain takes it in turn to select a boy to play for his team. Everybody knows who will be selected first: the boys who are in football teams out of school and are considered to be 'good' players. You hope to be picked somewhere in the middle but soon there is only you and one other boy left.

Summary

• Jamie's experience in the above example is probably similar to what millions of children have experienced in their early school days. However, the impact that this type of situation can have on an individual can be quite detrimental to their feelings about sport and future participation.

Questions

1 Was Jamie initially intrinsically or extrinsically motivated to play football?

2 Explain the types of things that could be seen as intrinsic and extrinsic motivators for a boy in this type of situation.

3 According to Cognitive Evaluation Theory, the type of feedback an individual receives can have an impact on their motivation. What types of feedback does Jamie receive in this situation?

4 How do you think the feedback Jamie receives may affect him in the future?

Achievement motivation

The importance of motivation in sport can be linked directly with an individual's desire to

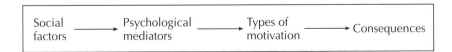

Figure 2.1: Sequence of motivation

achieve. An **achievement situation** was described by Atkinson (1964), who carried out much of the early work into this area, as 'one in which someone expects their performance to be evaluated', whilst **achievement motivation** is an athlete's predisposition to approach or avoid a competitive situation.

How does achievement motivation develop?

White (1959) believed that we are born with a competence motive (our need to confirm our sense of personal competence). This links in with Maslow's hierarchy of needs (see Chapter 1, page 2).

Veroff (1969) proposed that achievement motivation develops in three stages:

1 **Autonomous competence stage** – up to the age of about five, children are most concerned with mastering skills and aren't really interested in what others can do.
2 **Social comparison stage** – from about five or six, children start to compare themselves with others, i.e. they begin to use external standards. They are unlikely to progress to the next stage if they are uncomfortable in competitive situations. Those who are comfortable in competition and gain feedback about their performance are likely to progress.
3 **Integrated stage** – no fixed age. This is when the individual is able to use both autonomous competence and social comparison and knows when to use each one according to the situation. For example, a golfer might set personal goals and work towards those in practice, yet the same golfer will participate in competitions against others.

There are a number of theories that have been put forward to explain achievement motivation. Three will be examined in this chapter.

Theories of achievement motivation
The McClelland–Atkinson model

According to this theory, achievement motivation is based upon two psychological constructs:

- the motive to achieve success
- the fear of failure.

The motive to achieve success is representing the athlete's intrinsic motivation, whilst the fear of failure is a psychological construct associated with cognitive state anxiety (see pp. 26–7 for more details). Therefore, in its simplest form, the theory states that:

**achievement motivation =
intrinsic motivation – fear of failure**

It could be considered that the real value of measuring achievement motivation is in predicting long-term patterns of motivation rather than predicting success in a particular event.

The original McClelland–Atkinson model was not able to satisfactorily predict behaviour and therefore a number of additions to the model have been proposed. The first addition was the idea of extrinsic motivation, thus recognizing that some individuals are low in intrinsic motivation and high in fear of failure but still enter achievement situations. By including extrinsic motivation into the model, Atkinson is acknowledging that external factors may influence an individual's overall motivation.

The other aspect that the McClelland–Atkinson model is not able to explain is the difference between achievement motivation for men and women. The apparent lack of motivation to succeed in women competing with men led Horner (1968) to propose the psychological construct – fear of success (FOS). However, following a great deal of research into this construct the evidence for it is inconclusive. There is the possibility that for some female sports players, the reluctance to excel in certain achievement situations is probably due more to the traditionally masculine nature of the task – for example, playing football or rugby – than to the fear of success. Fear of success is not an independent personality trait. It is possible that as women are seen to be increasingly successful in society in general, it will have a positive effect on their participation in sports. RLA 8 looks at women's success and prominence at the Sydney Olympics 2000.

Commentary

A number of criticisms of the McClelland–Atkinson theory were made. One of these was criticism of the measurement, as concern has been expressed that assessment measures are unreliable (i.e. participants being asked to report their attitudes, and the use of anxiety scales). The relationship between achievement motivation and performance has also been questioned, as it is not clear exactly how the two link together.

Real Life Application 8:
Sydney's female form

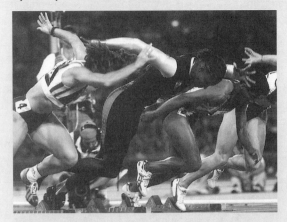

Aiming for gold at the Sydney Olympics

The Olympic Games in Sydney marked the centenary of women's involvement in the Olympics. In 1900, women were only allowed to compete in golf and tennis; in the 2000 Olympics, 38.4% of participants were female, which is a record. Women's sport has come a long way even in the last 30 years. In the 1970s, women's events were seen more as something to fill the time between the main men's events, yet in Sydney many of the men's events were overshadowed by the exciting performances of women such as Cathy Freeman, Marion Jones and Denise Lewis.

The image of women's events at the Olympics has changed over the years, moving away from the stereotypical 'masculine' female athletes towards a broader spectrum of female competitors. It is also now more common for women who have had children to continue training and return to international competition – for example, distance runner Sonia O'Sullivan.

Adapted from *The Observer*, 1 October 2000.

Summary

- It can be clearly seen that the prominence and image of women has changed over time in international competitions.
- It is thought that by the next Olympic Games, in Athens in 2004, the gap between the numbers of male and female participants will have narrowed even further.

Questions

1 What percentage of the participants at the Sydney Olympics were male?

2 How has the image of women's events in the Olympics changed over the years?

3 What effect do you think the increased prominence of the women at the Olympics will have generally on the likelihood of women approaching an achievement situation?

Self–confidence

As interest in the McClelland–Atkinson model declined due to its inability to consistently predict behaviour, interest in the concept of self-confidence rose. Researchers identified that the difference between individuals who rank high or low in achievement motivation is their level of self-confidence. For example, athletes who think that they will succeed are generally the ones who do. A number of theories were put forward exploring the notion of self–confidence. Bandura's theory of self-efficacy and Harter's theory of competence motivation will be considered next.

Bandura's theory of self-efficacy

Self-efficacy is an individual's belief that s/he is competent and is able to succeed at a particular task. According to Bandura's theory, the level of an individual's self-efficacy will determine whether that person will approach or avoid an achievement situation. Thus, the higher the levels of self-efficacy, the greater the enthusiasm to take part.

Bandura believed that there are four main factors that affect an individual's level of self-efficacy:

- past successful performance
- vicarious experience (watching others perform a task successfully will lead an individual to believe that they are more likely to be successful)
- verbal persuasion (encouragement from others)
- emotional arousal (how the individual interprets his/her feelings of arousal).

The most important factor is successful performance, which will increase self-efficacy, whilst failure will lead to a decrease. If an individual with high self-efficacy experiences an occasional failure this will not affect self-efficacy, which has been established due to repeated success. Experience of repeated success, through participatory modelling is, according to Bandura, absolutely crucial. This involves a participant observing a model performing a particular task; the model then helps the participant successfully perform the task, ensuring that the participant does not fail. Repeated experiences of success then lead to high levels of self-efficacy.

Jourden, Bandura and Banfield (1991) demonstrated the importance of self-efficacy when they showed that athletes who learnt a motor task, but believed that it was due to innate ability, showed little interest in the task. Those who believed that it was due to their own efforts developed a greater amount of self-efficacy.

Harter's competence motivation theory

Harter's theory also proposed that achievement motivation is based on a sport player's feeling of personal competence. Harter believed that individual's are innately motivated to be competent in all areas of human achievement. In order to achieve competency in sport, an individual attempts mastery. An individual's self-perception of these mastery attempts leads to either positive or negative feelings. Successful performance is likely to lead to high competence motivation and thus lead to more attempts at mastery of various tasks, whilst poor performance is likely to lead to low competence motivation, leading to fewer attempts at mastery and ultimately the possibility that the individual will drop-out of sport completely.

Harter also devised a way of measuring competence, the Perceived Competence Scale for Children (PCSC), which assesses the child's competence in three ways:

- cognitive
- social
- physical.

Much of the research carried out using this measure has found support for Harter's theory. Other research into the importance of developing competence motivation in sport has also lent support to Harter's ideas. For example, Weiss and Horn (1990) found that boys and girls who underestimate their own competence tend to be more likely to drop out of sports. The effect is, however, more damaging for girls. Children who assessed their own ability accurately felt more in control and thus sought involvement in challenging activities.

Commentary

The theories that are proposed by Bandura and Harter are based upon social and cognitive assumptions and therefore do not take into account other potential reasons for the differences in individuals' levels of motivation to participate in sport, such as developmental or physiological differences.

RLA 9 demonstrates how the motivation theories apply in real life sporting performances.

Real Life Application 9:
McRae's motivation

McRae competing in a rally

Colin McRae, a rally driver, was hoping to be world champion in 1998. He was viewed by other competitors as 'one to beat' and he had been particularly successful when completing the rallies in Britain. However, McRae's failure to complete the penultimate rally in Australia due to turbo failure ended his hopes of the title and meant waiting for the final rally, in Britain, to decide the championship between two other drivers. The failure to finish the Australian rally had a negative effect upon McRae's motivation. Initially he said he could not face the British event as his heart had been set on a second championship, and now that was not possible he felt the final rally meant nothing. He found it hard to accept that he was not in with a chance of the championship and therefore he felt he could not continue competing. He finally came to realize that he had to take part and once he started he would be concentrating on winning again.

Adapted from 'McRae holds the key to title' by David Allsop, *The Independent*, 21 November 1998.

Summary

- Even established successful sports competitors could lose motivation for periods of time if they believe that they are not achieving what they feel they ought to be.

Questions

1 How do you think Colin McRae's intrinsic and extrinsic motivation levels were affected by his failure in Australia?

2 How does the way Colin McRae was feeling after the Australia rally fit in with Bandura's theory of self-efficacy?

3 Why do you think McRae was able to go back to the rally and believe that he could win?

Gender differences in achievement motivation

As mentioned earlier, research has suggested that females have lower levels of achievement motivation than males. If this is the case, is it possible to alter these levels? Research, using Bem's (1974) Sex-Role Inventory to identify an individual's gender role as masculine, feminine or androgynous, has demonstrated that females who are characterized as masculine or androgynous showed higher levels of achievement motivation and self-confidence than females characterized as feminine.

Commentary

This finding suggests that in order to narrow the gender difference in achievement motivation levels, it would be beneficial for coaches to teach female sports players desirable masculine attributes and teach them how to utilize them in sporting situations.

Cross-cultural research – achievement motivation

The reference to achievement motivation in research that has been carried out in the West is connected to an individual's desire for excellence, and thus is closely linked with a tendency to push oneself forward and actively strive for and seek individual success. However, excellence may be sought through broader social goals, and this type of achievement motivation is found in societies where individuals have an interdependent sense of self, i.e. the aim to achieve excellence, fully acknowledging their connectedness with others.

Yang (1982) identified two forms of achievement motivation: individually orientated and socially orientated. Individual orientation in achievement motivation has been found predominantly in the West, and socially orientated achievement motivation is the much more common in societies that value collectiveness, such as China. Bond (1986) assessed the levels of various motivations in the Chinese and found that they showed much higher levels of socially orientated rather than individually orientated achievement motivation.

Doi (1985) examined achievement motivation in another interdependent culture, Japan. Japanese college students were asked 30 questions designed to measure tendencies to persevere and pursue excellence (achievement tendency) and 30 questions to measure desire to care for and be cared for by others (affiliation tendency). The results showed a very close association between the two. This is in contrast to general findings in the West, which indicate that the two dimensions are typically unrelated.

Thus the studies from China and Japan suggest that achievement motivation is closely linked to the social orientation of being connected to important others in life. This may help to explain in sport why societies who value collective effort rather than simply individual effort – for example, China and Russia – succeed in certain team events, such as gymnastics.

Commentary

The finding that achievement motivation is not the same in all cultures suggests that it is something that is influenced by the environment in which an individual is raised, rather than by innate tendencies. This may help to explain why certain nationalities are better at certain sports than others and possibly why people from very different cultures find it hard to work together.

Developing motivation and self-confidence

Gould, Hodge, Peterson and Giannini (1989) asked 101 successful wrestling coaches how they developed confidence in wrestlers and Weinberg and Jackson (1990) asked 222 high school tennis coaches how they developed confidence. Both studies found that the main ways for developing confidence were:

- the use of instruction-drilling
- encouraging the use of positive self-talk
- acting confident yourself (modelling confidence)
- the liberal use of praise statements
- hard physical conditioning.

It is possible to develop or enhance achievement motivation in children if they are allowed repeated experiences of success. Therefore, the winning needs to be de-emphasized and success needs to be viewed in terms of effort and improvement. This type of approach will lead to sport becoming a more positive experience.

Other ways of improving self-confidence include:

- goal setting throughout training, as the successful completion of a goal will lead to an increase in feelings of self-confidence
- using imagery (see Chapter 3) to visualize being confident and successful
- using positive self-talk – not focusing on any errors.

Arousal

What is arousal?

Arousal is the degree of activation of the organs and mechanisms that are under the control of the body's autonomic nervous system (ANS). As its name suggests, we do not have voluntary control over the organs and glands within the ANS – for example, we don't normally control heart rate, blood pressure and breathing. Arousal can be said to be our state of activation, ranging on a continuum, from deep sleep to extreme excitation.

Physiological signs of arousal

The autonomic nervous system has two divisions:

- sympathetic
- parasympathetic.

The sympathetic division is primarily responsible for the changes in bodily functions associated with arousal – for example, sweaty hands, increased heart rate, pupil dilation, increased respiration. It is also responsible for the release of glucose from the liver, decreased kidney output and the release of catecholamines – adrenaline and noradrenaline. The parasympathetic division selectively reduces the effects of the sympathetic division – for example, it slows down heart rate and constricts pupils.

The arousal reaction occurs as a result of a chain of events. Initially they start by your experience of certain sensory stimuli – for example, you hear the call for your 100-metres race at an athletics competition. The information goes to your ascending reticular activating system that sends information to your brain, about your perception of the situation. In your brain, the information goes to your hypothalamus and then to your cerebral cortex which in turn activates your sympathetic nervous system and leads to the release of adrenaline and noradrenaline into your bloodstream. This leads you to experience the sensation we know as physiological arousal.

The effect of arousal on the mind and body

Lacey (1967) identified three ways that arousal can affect us. Firstly an arousal reaction can affect the mind (electrocortisol arousal), the degree of electrical activity in the cortex can be measured by an EEG. The effects of arousal on the mind are shown by an increase in attention, faster processing of information, confused thinking and difficulty concentrating. Secondly, the arousal reaction can affect the body (autonomic arousal) and this can be identified by the degree of physiological activity in the autonomic nervous system, which is measured by skin conductance, heart rate and blood pressure. This increase in physiological activity is shown by sweaty palms and a pounding heart. Finally, arousal can affect our behaviour and this can be seen by observation and includes behaviour such as hands shaking and restless pacing.

Commentary

Whilst it can be seen that many of the effects of arousal could be considered to be negative, some effects will definitely enhance the performance of the sports player – for example, the increase in attention and faster processing of information.

Theories of arousal

It appears that some effects of arousal are positive, others are negative, and the impact this arousal might have on sporting performance therefore needs to be considered. In order to do this various theories need to be examined.

Drive theory

This is one of the earliest theories to be put forward to attempt to link an individual's arousal (drive) with his/her performance. Hull (1951) and Spence (1956) developed this theory and made the suggestion that if a skill is well learned, arousal will enable

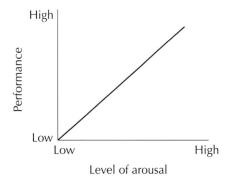

Figure 2.2: *The relationship between arousal and performance according to drive theory*

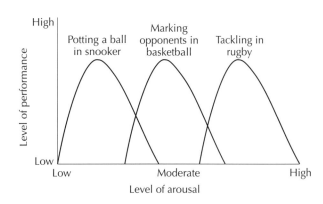

Figure 2.4: The optimum levels of arousal for different sporting skills

the individual to perform that skill well. However, if the skill is not well learned, arousal is likely to lead to a worse performance. Thus they suggested that performance = arousal x skill level (see Figure 2.2).

Spence and Spence (1966) reviewed twenty-five studies that investigated the arousal performance relationship and found that all but four supported the hypothesis that drive was positively correlated to performance.

Commentary

There have been a number of criticisms of this theory and other psychologists have found that there are also many studies that do not support the hypothesis. One of the main criticisms is what is meant by a well-learned task – this is very difficult to clearly define. This theory also offers no explanation for times when a sports player fails to succeed when performing a 'well-learned' task – for example, a striker missing a penalty in football.

Inverted U hypothesis

This hypothesis is able to offer some explanation for areas that drive theory could not explain. Based on the Yerkes–Dodson Law (1908), it predicts that arousal will lead to an increase in performance but

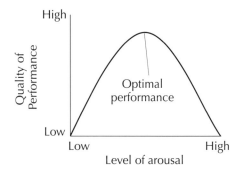

Figure 2.3: *The relationship between performance and arousal according to the inverted U theory*

only up to a point, beyond which further arousal will actually lead to a decline in performance. The shape of the curve leads to the title of the theory (see Figure 2.3). Hebb (1957) suggested there was an optimum level of arousal that would lead to an individual performing at his/her maximum potential.

Further research into the inverted U theory also allowed an explanation for the optimal performance point for sports requiring different skills. Oxendine (1970) noted that the level of arousal needed to reach optimal performance varied, depending upon the type of skill required. Complex skills, such as those requiring fine motor skills and co-ordination, have an optimal performance when levels of arousal are low, whilst more straightforward tasks, such as those requiring strength and endurance, benefit from higher levels of arousal (see Figure 2.4).

Commentary

The drawback with Oxendine's proposal is that many tasks involve both complex and strength skills and it would therefore be difficult to fit all tasks into this model.

Testing the inverted U theory

Research to test the proposals of the inverted U theory has looked at the effect of arousal on performance. Martens and Landers (1970) studied male junior high school students performing a motor task (a tracing task involving arm steadiness) under three controlled experimental conditions: low, moderate and high stress. In the low stress condition, no emphasis was placed on their scores, whilst in the high stress condition the participants were hooked up to shock machines with the threat of shocks for low scores. They found that the three conditions led to three different levels of arousal (measured both physiologically and by self-report) and their performance linked with the level of arousal led to an inverted U. Thus those in the moderate arousal condition performed better than those in the other two conditions.

Sonstroem and Bernardo (1982) carried out a field study with female university basketball players. They asked them to fill in questionnaires before the game to measure their anxiety, thus taking a measure of their arousal, and their performance was scored during the game. When comparing their pre-game anxiety and their performance, again an inverted U relationship was found.

Experienced sports players do not seem to suffer from drops in their performance to the same extent as novices. Is this because they do not experience the same amounts of arousal? Research – for example, Mahoney and Avener (1977) – suggests that experienced sportspeople still show increased levels of arousal. The difference, however, is that they can control the arousal much better than novices, and thus at the crucial moment will be experiencing near normal levels of arousal.

Commentary

Although the inverted U theory is able to explain phenomena that the drive theory couldn't, it is not able to explain fully the relationship between arousal and performance. Critics have made the point that it does not have very good predictive validity, as it appears that for most sports players arousal beyond the optimal point does not result in a gradual decline in performance, but rather a drastic decline. The inverted U theory has also been criticized for being reductionist, as it fails to take into account other factors that may affect the link between arousal and performance.

Alternatives to the inverted U theory

Due to the previous theory's inability to explain fully how arousal is linked to performance, psychologists have proposed alternatives to the inverted U theory. Two of these alternatives will be examined here: Hanin's (1980) Zone of Optimal Functioning and Fazey and Hardy's (1988) Catastrophe Theory. The more recent theories that have been put forward to explain arousal have also linked in the effects of anxiety. Some researchers use the terms almost interchangeably, yet whilst they are different entities, it is indisputable that arousal and anxiety are intertwined and often it is difficult to separate one from the other. In this chapter this has been done as far as is possible: however, as we can see from the following theories, it cannot be done completely.

Zone of optimal functioning

Following his study on élite female rowers, Hanin proposed the zone of optimal functioning (1980). He linked arousal and its effect on performance by measuring anxiety scores (as an indirect measure of arousal) and proposing individual zones of optimal functioning. Hanin studied 46 élite female rowers, measuring their levels of state anxiety (see pages 26–28 for more specific detail) just before competition and their subsequent performance. He found that the mean score for anxiety was 43.8 but the range was 26–67. The difficulty with this finding is that, as it is accepted that moderate amounts of anxiety appear to enhance performance, it is not possible, due the range of scores, to state what would be a 'moderate amount'. In order to judge what would be considered to be a moderate level, Hanin proposed that each sportsperson has a zone of optimal functioning (ZOF), which is their pre-state anxiety plus or minus 4 points. If the level of state anxiety falls within this zone then performance will be at its most effective. Therefore, the job of the coach is to identify the ZOF and help to control anxiety to within this zone.

Commentary

This theory is appealing as it acknowledges individual differences and it has extra strength due to the measurements taken.

Catastrophe theory

As the critics of the inverted U theory identified, performance does not always gradually deteriorate as arousal increases, there is sometimes a rapid decline – a catastrophe in performance. Fazey and Hardy (1988) therefore proposed the catastrophe theory. They were looking at the relationship between the anxiety that an individual experiences, the level of physiological arousal and the resultant effect on their performance. They believe that somatic and cognitive state anxiety (see page 26 for further details) do not just have different effects on performance but they also have an effect on each other.

Fazey and Hardy made a number of proposals within their catastrophe theory. Firstly, they suggested that the inverted U relationship applies to a performer with low levels of cognitive state anxiety, and increases in cognitive state anxiety will have a beneficial effect on performance if the performer is at a low level of physiological arousal. However, increases in cognitive state anxiety will have a detri-

A catastrophe in performance

mental effect on performance at high levels of physiological arousal. If cognitive state anxiety is high, then continuing increases in physiological arousal to a high level can cause a sudden and dramatic fall in performance – *the catastrophe*. If the catastrophe does occur, small reductions in arousal will not bring performance back to its previous level. The performer must relax, to reduce the arousal to below the point at which the catastrophe occurred.

In conclusion, Fazey and Hardy suggest that it is cognitive state anxiety linked to levels of physiological arousal that determines whether changes in sporting performance are gradual or dramatic.

Commentary

This theory is interesting because it acknowledges that arousal and anxiety do not always interact in an orderly fashion, rather when arousal levels become greater drastic changes can occur.

Competitiveness and anxiety

Earlier in this chapter we considered the issue of what motivates an individual to take part in a sporting activity. We will now take this a stage further by considering what is meant by competition and how an individual may demonstrate competitiveness and how, linking with arousal (see page 22), this can lead to anxiety.

What is competition?

One definition of competition is that it is 'a process in which the comparison of an individual's performance is made with some standard in the presence of at least one other person who is aware of the criterion for comparison and can evaluate the comparison process' (Martens, 1977). According to Martens, competition is nothing more than a sports-specific achievement situation. Competition is goal-directed (the goal being superior performance) and rivalry is person directed. Thus competitiveness can be said to be 'to strive for satisfaction when making comparisons with some standard of excellence in the presence of evaluative others in sport' (Martens, 1977). Therefore, competitiveness can be seen as a sport-specific form of achievement motivation. Competitiveness develops from achievement motivation.

Measuring competitiveness

As competitiveness is concerned with an individual striving for excellence and comparing oneself with others, it may be quite hard to ascertain whether a sports player is very competitive or only moderately competitive. Gill and Deeter (1988) attempted to find a way to measure it and they developed the Sport Orientation Questionnaire (SOQ) to measure individuals' competitiveness and competition behaviour.

The questionnaire has 25 questions and measures 3 dimensions:

- competitiveness – desire to seek and strive for success in sport-specific situations
- win orientation – desire to win competitive sporting events
- goal orientation – desire to reach personal goals in sport.

In order to discover the usefulness of the SOQ, they carried out a comparison of athletes and non-athletes and of male and female athletes that led to the following conclusions:

- men scored consistently higher than women on competitiveness and win orientation
- women generally scored a little higher on goal orientation
- athletes scored higher than non-athletes on most dimensions.

Commentary

This would suggest that if athletes were scoring more highly than non-athletes the questionnaire is useful and has some validity for measuring competitiveness, as you would expect athletes to be more competitive than non-athletes.

Cross-cultural research – competitiveness

Another way that it is possible to double-check

methods of measuring competitiveness is by carrying out cross-cultural studies. Nelson and Kagan (1972) studied children from different countries and from different areas within those countries. They found that:

- American children were more competitive than Mexican children
- urban children in a number of countries were more competitive than rural children
- highly competitive children gave up the chance of a reward for themselves in order to keep other children from getting similar rewards.

They proposed that cultural differences in competitiveness are linked to child-rearing patterns. For example, American mothers reward their children according to the child's achievement, whereas Mexican mothers praise and encourage their children regardless of outcome.

Orlick (1978) carried out a further cross-cultural study. The study aimed to introduce co-operative broomball to urban children in southern Canada and to Inuit children in the Northwest Territories. The game had no goalkeepers, goals counted for the other team and after scoring a goal the player changed teams. The findings were that:

- Northern Canadian children were more positive about the game
- girls reacted more positively than boys to co-operative games
- younger children were more positive than the older children.

Commentary

These cross-cultural studies would seem to suggest that competitiveness is something that is developed during people's upbringings rather than something that is present to the same degree in everyone from birth. This leads to the conclusion that competitiveness is due to nurture not nature.

Anxiety

Having now considered what is meant by competitiveness, and earlier in this chapter, how arousal links in to sport, it is now important to consider the effect that too much of either can have on sporting performance. In order to do this we will examine the issue of anxiety.

Arousal itself is neutral but if we associate it with negative thoughts we experience anxiety. In its simplest form anxiety can be described as a 'subjective feeling of apprehension and heightened physiological arousal' (Levitt, 1980).

According to Endler (1978) there are five parts to anxiety:

1 interpersonal ego threat – threat to self-esteem as a result of failure
2 physical danger – threat of personal harm
3 ambiguity – unpredictability and fear of the unknown
4 disruption of daily routine – fear of change to daily habits
5 social evaluation – fear of being negatively evaluated by others.

What is competitive anxiety?

Competitive anxiety is the motive to avoid failure in a sport-specific setting, or the tendency to become anxious and worried about failure in sport. A great deal of the work carried out within sports psychology has focused on individual differences in competitive anxiety and ways of reducing anxiety. Some sportspeople become physically ill before a game, whilst others remain very calm.

Commentary

For individual sports players it is therefore important to work out what situations make them feel anxious, and thus aim to control their anxiety. It is also essential that coaches treat all sports players as individuals.

Theoretical basis of competitive anxiety

Rainier Martens has carried out a great deal of research to enable him to develop a theory and a test for competitive anxiety. His work has been built around four main principles:

1 **Interaction approach** – he believes that there is a strong interaction of personality and situational factors in sport.
2 **State–trait anxiety distinction** – Spielberger (1971) further developed the interaction approach by distinguishing between the rela-

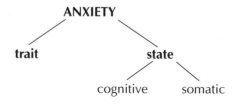

Figure 2.5: Types of anxiety

tively stable personality characteristic of trait anxiety (see Chapter 1 on personality) and the immediate, changeable feelings associated with state anxiety. Figure 2.5 illustrates how anxiety can be sub-divided. Definitions of each subdivision are given below.

Trait anxiety is considered to be a feature of personality that is a predisposition to perceive certain environmental stimuli as threatening. **State anxiety**, however, is the immediate emotional state that is characterized by apprehension, fear and tension accompanied by physical arousal. State anxiety has been further sub-divided and **cognitive state anxiety** is the mental component of state anxiety which is linked to the fear of negative self-evaluation and threat to self-esteem, whilst **somatic state anxiety** is directly related to physiological arousal.

3 **General v. specific anxiety** – highly trait anxious people tend to become anxious in all stressful situations but this isn't always equal. Therefore a situation-specific measure of trait anxiety is more useful for predicting state anxiety than a general measure of trait anxiety. Martens believed that a measure of sport-specific trait anxiety would be the best way of predicting state anxiety in sport competitions. He therefore proposed the idea of competitive trait anxiety.

4 **Competition** – Martens proposed a model of the competitive process which looked at the idea of competition being a process for comparison of sporting ability and therefore the main source of situational anxiety comes from the evaluation of our performance.

Martens, Vealey and Burton (1990) propose that anxiety has three components:

* cognitive state anxiety – worrying and experiencing negative thoughts
* somatic state anxiety – perception of bodily symptoms
* self-confidence – expectations of success or failure.

They developed the Competitive State Anxiety Inventory (CSAI and CSAI-2) to measure these. This included items such as:

* I am concerned that I may not do as well in this competition as I could
* my heart is racing
* I'm concerned that I won't be able to concentrate.

Participants had to say for each of the items whether they experienced it not at all, somewhat, moderately or very much.

How can each aspect of anxiety affect our performance?

Somatic state anxiety – an example of how this may be displayed is the athlete who 'froze' on the starting blocks. Many sportspeople show muscle tension or poor co-ordination when they experience high levels of state anxiety. Those who already have a high level of trait anxiety will display more state anxiety. An example of this is a study carried out by Weinberg and Hunt (1976) with two groups of students: high and low trait anxious. The students had to throw a tennis ball at a target, their accuracy was observed and the electrical activity in their muscles was monitored. They found that high trait anxious students showed more somatic state anxiety and used more energy. The increase in anxiety affected their performance.

Cognitive state anxiety includes the fear of failure, difficulties in attention and concentration, faulty decision-making and worries about performance. Ziegler (1978) believes that cognitive state anxiety can create a negative cycle (see Figure 2.6).

The link between different anxieties

Burton (1988) studied swimmers and found that optimal performance was when somatic state anxiety was moderate and cognitive state anxiety was low (see Figure 2.7).

Gender differences and anxiety

Research has again identified gender differences when looking at levels of anxiety. For example, a study by Anderson and Williams (1987) classified male and female sports participants as either feminine, masculine or androgynous and looked at the relationship between their gender type and their

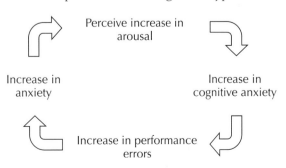

Figure 2.6: The negative cycle created by anxiety

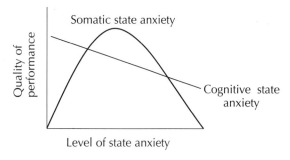

Figure 2.7: The link between different anxieties for swimmers

anxiety levels. Their levels of anxiety were measured via a self-report questionnaire devised by Martens, the Sport Competition Anxiety Test (SCAT). They found that the greatest degree of competitive trait anxiety was demonstrated by feminine females and the lowest level was shown by masculine males.

Commentary

The findings from this study may suggest that feminine females, who suffer most from anxiety, may be most likely to avoid or drop out of sport. Therefore if coaches can identify participants' gender role orientation, they may be able to train participants appropriately and thus encourage feminine females to take part.

Anxiety and timing

Numerous studies have looked at the relationship between time to the event and state anxiety (see Key Study 4).

KEY STUDY 4

Researchers: Gould, Petlichkoff and Weinberg (1984)

Aim: To examine levels of anxiety before competitions and identify any differences between cognitive and somatic anxiety.

Method: They studied two groups of sports participants: wrestlers and volleyball players. In the first study, 37 élite wrestlers were given the CSAI-2 before 2 major competitions. In the second study, 63 female high school volleyball players were given the CSAI-2 on 5 different occasions: 1 week before, 48 hours before, 24 hours before, 2 hours before and 20 minutes

---

before major tournaments.

Results: They found that somatic anxiety increased during the time leading up to the competition, whilst cognitive anxiety and confidence remained constant. They did not find support in this study for differences in anxiety between different abilities of players.

Conclusions: It has been found that cognitive anxiety starts high and remains so, whilst somatic anxiety starts quite low and only begins to increase as the event gets close. This could, therefore, be useful when training sports players, to manage their anxiety.

Measurement of anxiety

We can see from the studies that we have looked at that it is possible to attempt to measure anxiety in a number of ways. Table 2.1, on the next page, lists some of the main ones.

Commentary

It is important to remember that whilst there are a range of ways of measuring anxiety there are potential drawbacks concerning their accuracy. Although physiological measures are objective, knowing that a measurement is being taken may affect an individual's reading. Self-report measures offer a good opportunity to gain a real 'insight' into the way a sports player is feeling; however, they rely on the individual telling the truth and there will always be the issue of whether every individual interprets the questions in the same way. Behavioural observations can serve as a useful check to support the other two but, as ever with observation, it is necessary to ensure that inter-observer reliability is checked and, whenever possible, to carry out 'blind' observations.

Techniques for reducing arousal and anxiety

There are a range of different ways that coaches and sports players can aim to reduce arousal and anxiety levels. In order for any technique to be effective it is necessary to reverse the arousal/anxiety spiral. Somatic techniques can be very effective at reducing arousal and subsequent anxiety levels. They focus

Type of measure	Example
Physiological measures (measures of arousal, but also used as measures of anxiety)	• Electroencephalogram (EEG) • Electrocardiogram (ECG) • Electromynogram (EMG) • Galvanic skin response • Sudorimeter
Self-report questionnaires	• State, Trait Anxiety Inventory – Spielberger (1977) • Cognitive Somatic Anxiety Questionnaire (CSAQ) – Schwartz, Davidson and Neal (1978) • Sport Competition Anxiety Test (SCAT) – Martens (1977) • Competitive State Anxiety Inventory (CSAI and CSAI-2) – Martens (1982, 1990)
Behavioural observation	• Checklist for monitoring behavioural responses of the athlete – Harris and Harris (1984) • Direct observation

Table 2.1: Different ways of measuring anxiety

on reducing the physiological feelings associated with arousal and anxiety. Cognitive techniques can also be effective and these focus on changing the way the mind perceives the arousal sensation as anxiety.

Somatic techniques

Three somatic techniques will be considered here:

- progressive relaxation
- meditation
- biofeedback.

Progressive relaxation

This technique was originally started by Jacobson (1929, 1938) and involves systematically tensing and relaxing the muscles. Whilst it can take months of training to perfect the technique, once accomplished a sportsperson should be able to relax in a few minutes. Research has found that this can effectively reduce anxiety, yet it is more effective in conjunction with other techniques.

Meditation

As a relaxation technique, meditation is closely linked to selective attention (see Chapter 3, page 32), as it requires the individual to focus attention on a single thought or object. The use of meditation is more successful for tasks requiring the use of gross motor skills than those requiring fine motor skills.

Biofeedback

The technique of biofeedback involves an individual learning to control the responses of their autonomic nervous system. It is a relatively modern technique and rather than learning to relax, as with the other techniques, it involves reducing the physiological responses that are leading to increased arousal. Many studies have found that sportspeople who use biofeedback do become less aroused and anxious.

Another somatic technique is learning to control breathing and in particular the use of deep breathing. This is one of the easiest ways of reducing the levels of arousal.

Cognitive techniques

Three cognitive techniques will be considered:

- imagery
- goal setting
- self-talk.

Imagery

Imagery (see Chapter 3, pages 35–8, for further detail) is often used in conjunction with relaxation techniques to reduce feelings of anxiety. The use of imagery techniques will enable sports players to reduce the feelings of arousal, due to the fact that as they run through the event in their minds their feelings of self-efficacy will increase. Page, Sime and Nordell (1999) found that when they gave 40 female swimmers imagery techniques to utilize, they actually demonstrated a reduction in their perception of their anxiety.

Goal setting

The use of goal setting should help the sports player to focus away from their anxiety and towards the goals they are aiming for. When using goal setting it is important that to attempt to reduce feelings of stress, the goals that are set are performance related rather than output related. It is also important that the goals set are relatively short term and attainable, otherwise greater levels of anxiety may be created.

Self-talk

This technique involves individuals 'talking to them themselves'. It can be positive, helping to reduce arousal and anxiety and improve concentration or performance, or negative, leading to further feelings of anxiety, frustration and distraction. Positive self-talk involves individuals focusing themselves – for example, saying to themselves, 'watch the ball', or 'keep running, I can score a goal'. Whilst negative self-talk can be quite destructive – for example, 'I've no chance now' or 'there is no point trying, he always gets to the ball faster than I do'. It is therefore important that if this is to be used as a technique to reduce anxiety, sports players must learn how to 'self-talk' positively.

Therefore we can see that there are a range of different techniques that sports players can use to aim to control or reduce arousal and anxiety levels. RLA 10 examines how techniques can work in practice.

Tony Jarrett in 110m hurdles

gold medal. In the final 'nerves' threatened his performance. It was seven minutes between the field coming to the blocks and getting away cleanly, following two false starts, one by Jarrett. He said that he was getting over-excited at the start and was saying to himself that this could be his gold! He knew that he had to step away and take a deep breath. Once the race started Jarrett had an untidy race, clipping five of the ten hurdles and lunged over the line. The result – he won the gold medal.

Adapted from 'Jarrett clatters way to overdue gold' by Mike Rowbottom, *The Independent*, 21 September 1998.

Summary

- The way that Tony Jarrett felt after not winning a medal at the European Championships highlights again how even accomplished athletes can suffer from lapses in self-confidence.
- When competing in the Commonwealth Games, Jarrett had to draw on techniques he has learnt to ensure that he was focused enough to win the race.

Real Life Application 10:

Jarrett clatters to gold

Tony Jarrett was so disappointed by his failure to win the 110 metres hurdles in the European Championships in the summer of 1998 that he locked himself away and didn't speak to anyone for two days. After words of encouragement from his sister he realized he should start training and competing again. He won his semi-final in the Commonwealth Games and was aiming for the

Questions

1 Why do you think that Tony Jarrett was responsible for one of the false starts?

2 What was the point of stepping aside and taking a deep breath?

3 What type of technique is deep breathing?

Essay questions

1 With reference to theories, discuss how you could aim to improve motivation and self-confidence in young sports players.

2 Describe and evaluate what psychologists have discovered about how arousal links to sporting performance.

3 There are a range of ways of measuring anxiety in sport, the three main types being: physiological measures, self-report measures and behavioural observation. Evaluate the usefulness of each of these for measuring anxiety.

3 Cognitive psychology and sport

The focus of this chapter is how our mental processes can influence our behaviour and potentially our sporting behaviour. It considers whether successful sportspeople utilize different cognitive strategies than other sports players. The following areas will be considered: attentional style, the use of imagery, and the attributions that people make both for their own and other people's behaviour. Real Life Applications that are considered are:

- RLA 11: Strategies for rowers
- RLA 12: Imagery in rugby
- RLA 13: Attribution training and achievement in sport.

Cognitive style and sport

The following section is going to look at individual differences in cognitive skills as it is generally believed that certain cognitive skills have an effect on sporting performance. These include such skills as attentional style, memory and concentration.

The focus on cognitive skills raises the nature–nurture debate, as psychologists aim to ascertain whether these individual differences are due to innate personality differences (see Chapter 1) or whether the differences are due to an individual's upbringing or even their sports coaching.

Attentional style

Attention is concerned with focusing the mind to deal with certain things. In relation to attention and sport, research is generally concerned with two main factors:

- selectivity
- alertness.

Selectivity is concerned with how players limit attention to selected objects – for example, whether an individual can pick out an 'open' player for a pass and whether they are able to pick up on cues from others.

Alertness is how keen players' cognitive attention is – for example, whether they are paying attention to the starting signal and whether they are able to concentrate at the end of a tiring event.

In order to investigate attentional style further and identify any individual differences, Nideffer developed an Attentional Model (1976). He proposed that attentional style varied along two dimensions:

- width
- direction.

According to Nideffer, width ranged from broad (taking in a wide range of cues from the surrounding environment) to narrow (focusing upon only a limited range of factors). Direction varied from internal (attention is focused on factors/feelings within your own body) to external (attention is more focused on events or objects outside of the body).

Nideffer, therefore, was suggesting that there are four types of attentional style, which are shown in Table 3.1, on the following page. A broad–external attentional style is useful when players want to take in a large amount of information, whilst having a broad–internal attentional style is useful for planning and analysing previous performances. A narrow–external attentional style is appropriate for activities that require concentration, possibly on an object or ball, and a narrow–internal attentional style is useful for mental rehearsal or for performing strength or endurance tasks.

All of these attentional focuses can be useful on different occasions and relying on only one can lead to problems. Therefore, ideally, a sports player should be able to switch between the different atten-

	External	*Internal*
Broad	Broad–external (can be used in any sport to check the positions of other players)	Broad–internal (would be used for planning tactics and could be used by coaches)
Narrow	Narrow–external (a style that is useful for sports requiring concentration: for example golf)	Narrow–internal (often used for endurance sport players such as weightlifters)

Table 3.1: Four different types of attentional style

tional styles, depending on the requirements of each particular situation.

Nideffer also introduced the notion of cognitive overload, which occurs when an individual has too much information to process at any one time. He argues that changes in arousal levels can lead to changes in attention and concentration. Consequently, performance may be affected in a number of ways. For example, the sports player scans the field less often and other players may then take him/her by surprise, he/she may attend to the wrong cues, such as the crowd, which will again lead to a decrease in performance.

Nideffer also classified people as either effective or ineffective attenders.

Effective attenders:
- do not become overloaded
- can deal with several pieces of information simultaneously
- can easily switch between the different attentional styles.

Ineffective attenders:
- do not concentrate well
- tend to become overloaded and confused
- cannot narrow their attention effectively, it is either narrowed too much or not enough.

Measuring attentional style

In order to assess the effects that differences in attentional style may have on sporting performance we need to be able to measure it. Landers (1988) identified three main methods of measurement. Firstly, there is behavioural assessment where the measure used is generally reaction time. Secondly, it is possible to use physiological indicators; this would be carried out in the same way as the measurement of arousal (see Chapter 2). Alternatively, it

is possible to measure attentional style using self-report measures, most commonly in the form of a questionnaire. Behavioural assessment and physiological indicators tend to measure attentional abilities at a specific point in time whereas the self-report measure is more of an indicator of attentional focus as a personality disposition.

Nideffer, using college students as his subjects, developed a self-report inventory called the Test of Attentional and Interpersonal Style (TAIS). This has 17 variables, of which 6 subscales measure attentional processes. High scores on Broad–External (BET), Broad–Internal (BIT) and Narrow Effective focus (NAR) reflect positive attentional traits. High scores on Overload of External Information (OET), Overload of Internal Information (OIT) and Reduced Attention (RED) reflect negative attentional traits.

Commentary

The TAIS has been criticized by other psychologists as having insufficient predictive validity (scores on the test do not enable predictions to be made about the future performance of an individual). Nideffer has said that basically it is a personality inventory that may generate some useful information about attentional style. Landers (1985) found the TAIS to be an unreliable predictor of sporting performance and suggested that this type of research should rely less on questionnaires and make greater use of behavioural and physiological measures.

Alternatives to the TAIS

In view of the criticisms that have been made about the TAIS, it is worth considering why it seems not to predict performance. One possible reason is that it is not sport- or situation-specific, thus other psychologists have since tried to develop self-report measures of attentional style that are more directly related to sport and in some cases specifically for one particular sport. These have been found to have greater predictive validity than the TAIS. For example, Van Schoyk and Grasha (1981) developed the tennis TAIS (T-TAIS) and gave both Nideffer's original TAIS and their T-TAIS to 90 tennis players, with an equal number of male and female players. They found that the tennis-specific test had better predictive validity and greater test–retest reliability.

Attentional style and performance

Having considered the possible ways of measuring attentional style, we will now look at the main use for the information this generates, which is to investigate the link between attentional style and sporting performance.

Association/dissociation

One distinction that has been made in the types of attentional style utilized is that of association/dissociation. Sports players who use an associative strategy use an internal attentional focus, concentrating on their breathing, the feelings in their muscles and other signals from their body. Those using a dissociative strategy focus externally and block out feedback from the body. Morgan and Pollock (1977) carried out a study looking at 27 marathon runners

A marathon runner

and their attentional style. They found that some runners were associaters and some were dissociaters. Elite runners used associative strategies, leading to the suggestion that a narrow–internal attentional style was beneficial for endurance sports.

Other research has been carried out to investigate Morgan and Pollock's findings. Morgan et al (1988) studied élite runners and found that 72% reported using an associative technique during competition and 28% reported using both. However, during training 21% used an associative technique, 43% used a dissociative strategy and 36% used both. Thus, this seems to be suggesting that élite performers are able to switch between different attentional styles as required and that they have developed an ability to block out bodily signals when training yet rely heavily on them when actually performing.

Gill and Strom (1985) studied female athletes doing an endurance task at the gym. They were divided into two groups: narrow–internal attentional style, who were told to focus on the feelings in their legs, and narrow–external attentional style, who were focusing on a picture. They found that those using narrow–external completed more repetitions. Pennebaker and Lightner (1980) showed that distraction led to better performance in two experiments. Firstly, individuals exercising on a treadmill reported less fatigue when distracted than when focusing on their own breathing and secondly, individuals ran faster on a cross-country course where there were distractions than when they ran laps on a running track.

Masters and Ogles (1998) reviewed the literature (35 articles in total) on the use of associative and dissociative strategies. Much of the work had been carried out with runners and they found that generally associative techniques correlated with faster running, with racers preferring to use association and distance runners using dissociation. However, both types of runner use both techniques.

Commentary

It appears that both techniques can be beneficial for different individuals and in different situations. However, it is important to remember that some of the research findings have come from controlled experiments looking at only one sport, leading to potential problems with representitiveness. More research is needed to investigate the extent to which the styles can be manipulated.

Whilst it can be seen that certain athletes tend to use various combinations of the strategies, RLA 11 examines whether it is advantageous to favour a particular technique.

Real Life Application 11:

Strategies for rowers

The suggestion from the research seems to be that élite athletes benefit from using association, so should novices try to use dissociation? Scott, Scott, Bedic and Dowd (1999) investigated this idea using nine novice rowers as their participants. They were assigned to one of three experimental conditions and had to row, on a rowing machine, as far as they could in forty minutes. One group, the associative condition, were played a tape of their cox giving instructions while they were rowing, a second group, dissociative (music), listened to a tape of pop music and the third group, dissociative (video), watched the 1992 rowing championships while they rowed. Their performance was compared with a previously measured baseline performance and they found that those using the associative technique demonstrated the greatest increase in performance.

Scott, Scott, Bedic and Dowd (1999).

Summary

- This study suggests that novices may benefit from using associative strategies and this could therefore have implications for coaches.
- It would also be useful to examine this finding further as the sample used in this study was very small.

Questions

1 Why did the experimenters have three experimental conditions, with two connected to rowing and one with pop music?

2 How could coaches use this information in training sessions?

Thought stopping

From the evidence presented in this chapter it is possible to see that attentional style is important and an inability to switch between the different styles may lead to a reduction in sporting performance. It is important that sportspeople are able to focus their attention to stop negative thoughts and this requires them to develop a high degree of attentional control. The process of stopping a negative thought and replacing it with a positive one is known as 'thought stopping'. Directing thoughts internally is known as 'centring'. Following centring the athlete can attend narrowly to a relevant external cue and then carry out the skilled action.

Developing the ability to use the techniques of thought stopping and centring is not easy and will therefore develop within a sports player over time. It could be a particular focus for the coach to assist his/her players to develop and utilize the techniques.

Imagery

The technique of imagery involves the use of visualization to imagine situations. It is useful for relaxation and reducing anxiety and it can also be used to allow rehearsal in sporting situations and thus improve performance. Although the notion of imagery is not new – the first ever research into mental imagery being carried out by Galton in 1883 – as with any cognitive technique, there are great individual differences with regard to the use and success of imagery. It is now becoming an increasing popular area for research within sports psychology.

There are two main types of imagery:

- internal
- external.

Internal imagery is when you imagine yourself doing something and thus experience the sensations

Linford Christie preparing for a race using imagery techniques

involved in carrying out that act – for example, athletes preparing themselves for field events such as javelin. External imagery, however, is imagining seeing yourself doing something as though you are watching yourself carrying out the act on film – for example, Formula 1 racing drivers rehearsing the route before a race.

Initial research suggested that internal imagery was best for sport performance (for example, Mahoney and Avener (1977) studying gymnasts). However, it is now thought that some combination of both may facilitate the best performance. It has been shown that a physiological difference exists between the two types, with internal imagery generating greater muscle activity than external imagery. For example, Hale (1982) studied weightlifters and found that those who used internal imagery experienced greater biceps muscle activity than those who used external imagery.

Measurement of imagery ability

Whilst it is relatively simple to identify what imagery is, in order for it be appropriately utilized in sport, it is important to be able to measure it accurately. By measuring imagery it allows coaches and sports players to be able to discover how best to put it into practice. Moran (1993) reviewed the literature on imagery assessment and discovered that a range of measures are available, most are however self-report measures. Although there are a variety of different measures they do not all measure the same aspect of imagery. The early measures were more concerned with the vividness of the imagery – for example, Questionnaire on Mental Imagery (QMI) by Betts (1908), which was shortened by Sheehan in 1967. Other measures over the years have focused on particular aspects of imagery, such as preferred style and control, but the more recently developed measures acknowledge the interaction of various factors connected with imagery and are therefore multi-dimensional. Examples of these include the Imagery Use Questionnaire (IUQ) developed by Hall, Rodgers and Barr (1990) and the Sport Imagery Questionnaire (SIQ) developed by Hall, Mack and Paivio (1996).

Commentary

Although there have been a number of attempts to devise a way of measuring imagery, none can be said to be perfect. Unfortunately, none of the self-report scales are able to consistently predict the effect imagery may have on performance. The drawback with these self-report measures is that they are reliant on honesty from the sports players. It is also possible that individual interpretation of the questions varies and if the questionnaires are completed after the use of imagery the sports player is dependent on their memory for specific details about their feelings.

Imagery and sport performance

The research into this area is relatively sparse and rather inconclusive, partly for the reasons mentioned above. However, Feltz and Landers (1983) reviewed literature and found that when mental rehearsal is combined with physical rehearsal, performance improves compared to just physical rehearsal. Mental training is particularly effective for skills with a large cognitive component – for example, those requiring a long sequence, such as gymnastics and those involving decision-making and strategies.

There are a number of possible reasons why this type of situation might lead to the optimum utilization of imagery:

- It enables the performer to try out different strategies and correct faults by replaying the events in their own mind.
- The sportsperson is able to practise their performance without the risk of public failure.
- Using imagery avoids the arousal caused by performing in front of others and thus prevents this having a detrimental effect on performance.
- Imagery may allow an injured sports player to keep on top of their skills when they are unable to perform.
- The neuromuscular system is slightly activated when using imagery and it is therefore a weak form of physical training.

Some research has found indicating that imagery does improve sporting performance (see Key Study 5).

KEY STUDY 5

Researchers:	Hall, Rodgers and Barr (1990)
Aim:	To investigate the use of imagery across a variety of sports.
Method:	In order to measure use of imagery in sport, they questioned (using the Imagery Use Questionnaire) sports players from six different sports: football, ice-hockey, squash,

gymnastics, skating and American football. The players were also categorized according to their skill level in an attempt to identify any link between skill level and imagery.

Results: General findings were that sports players used imagery extensively, particularly in competitions, and that they visualized themselves winning, never losing. They found that internal and external imagery were used equally amongst all players. However, as skill level increased so did the use of imagery.

Conclusions: This study illustrates that the use of imagery in sport is widespread and possibly improves with practice, as the more skilful players used imagery more frequently.

Isaac (1992) carried out a further study looking at the use of imagery in sport. This study focused on only one sport, trampolining, and found that those who used imagery improved their motor skills more than those who did not use imagery. High imagers improved their skills more than those rated as low imagers. Again there appears to be a link between skill level and imagery, with the more experienced trampolinists benefiting more from the use of imagery.

Acquiring the ability to use imagery techniques can also be beneficial to team performances as RLA 12 demonstrates.

Real Life Application 12:

Imagery in rugby

In 1998, Sheffield Eagles beat all the odds and won Rugby League's Challenge Cup Final against Wigan 17–8. Sheffield were the underdogs nobody expected to win. Coach John Kear explained after the game that the decisive moment in their victory had come the night before in their hotel. What Kear is referring to is the mental preparation that the team undertook. He describes how he had them all in a circle and asked them to

Sheffield Eagles celebrate their victory

tell the rest of the team what they were prepared to do the following day. The atmosphere was electric and he believes that they knew then that they were going to win. Kear was assisted in preparing the team by Barry Johnson who was part of the Castlefield team who had a surprise win in the same competition in 1986. He was able to share his experience, starting with how it felt to walk out of the tunnel. Kear goes on to explain that as a result of this the whole team had mentally rehearsed walking out of the tunnel, meeting the dignitaries and completing their kick-off drills. The team had played the game in their heads the day before and knew exactly what they were going to do. This mental rehearsal led the team to develop a unity of belief that 1998 was Sheffield Eagles' year. Even in the tunnel before the game the Eagles were shouting '98' to keep them focused and stop everything getting to them and to give Wigan something to think about.

Adapted from *The Guardian*, 4 May 1998.

Summary

- Sheffield Eagles' 1998 victory highlights how performance can be enhanced by appropriate mental preparation.
- The team were seen has having virtually no chance of winning yet, through imagery they had built up such a sense of self-belief that they did not think they could fail.

Questions

1 Do you think that a particular attentional style would benefit the players in Sheffield Eagles team? Give reasons for your answer.

2 Why was it important that the whole team was together while they carried out their mental preparation?

3 What type of imagery were the Eagles using?

Developing imagery skills

Research has shown that imagery skills can be improved through training – for example, Rodgers, Hall and Buckolz's (1991) study of figure skaters.

It is possible for coaches to train sports players in the use of imagery to a certain extent. Wann (1997) suggested that there are a number of ways that imagery skills can be developed. Below is a list of the key points.

- Try to relax and find a quiet setting.
- Develop vivid images, using colour, and if possible draw on past experiences to help develop the image.
- Make use of as many senses as possible. Imagine seeing the ball, feeling the shot, hearing the crowd.
- Experiment with internal and external imagery and find which works best. It is possible to use a combination of both.
- Believe in the usefulness of imagery and it will be more effective.
- Evaluate the use of imagery and, where necessary, make alterations to the techniques.

Attributions of self and others

As individuals we are constantly trying to explain the behaviour of both others and ourselves. If we are able to identify the causes of behaviour it will help us to predict what people may do in the future. Attributions are the perceived causes of a particular outcome and can be internal or external. Internal causes include individual differences such as personality characteristics and abilities, whilst external causes originate outside of the individual – for example, environmental and social pressures. In football, a goalkeeper fails to make a save. An internal cause may be that he lacks ability as a goalkeeper, whilst an external cause may be that he was distracted by the noise of the crowd.

Commentary

Our attributions and those of others can have an impact on sporting performance, as the way in which the cause of the behaviour is attributed will affect how the sportsperson feels about his/her performance and thus the extent to which self-esteem is affected.

The attribution process

Heider (1944, 1958) is acknowledged as the founder of attribution theory. His basic suggestion was that behavioural outcome was composed of two factors: personal forces (internal forces, sub-divided into ability and effort) and impersonal forces (environmental factors, sub-divided into task difficulty and luck). Thus, according to Heider, the internal and environmental causes of behaviour are additive and therefore at its simplest:

behavioural outcome = personal force + impersonal force

Weiner (1972, 1979) developed Heider's basic idea further. He restructured Heider's four main factors and defined two main causal dimensions: locus of control (sub-divided into internal and external attributions) and stability (sub-divided into stable and unstable attributions).

Internal and external attributions relate to the notion of locus of control (Rotter, 1971). An individual with an internal locus of control tends to believe that their own behaviour is influencing outcomes, whilst an individual with an external locus of control believes that the outcome is due to outside factors, such as luck or fate.

Stable and unstable attributions are based on past experience and therefore create expectations about the future. Stable attributions are likely to stay the same over time, whilst unstable attributions may vary from time to time and from situation to situation.

Table 3.2 summarizes the combinations of the dimensions of attribution with the way that Heider's attributions fit into Weiner's dimensions.

In order to understand how different attributions can be made, consider the example of a gold-medal-winning, 400-metres male runner who comes third

		Locus of control	
		Internal	*External*
Stability	*Stable*	ability	task difficulty
	Unstable	effort	luck

Table 3.2: Types of attribution

in a race. He may attribute not winning to the weather being too hot (unstable–external), or he may believe that his opponents were much better than he was (stable–external). Alternatively, he may say that he didn't really try his best (unstable–internal) or he could believe that he does not have the ability to win any more and even in another race would be unable to come first (stable–internal). The type of attribution that the runner makes will have an impact on how it affects his performance. If not winning is attributed to stable–internal factors the athlete will believe that there is little that he can do to change, whereas if he attributes it to a lack of effort there is scope for improvement in the future.

Controllability and learned helplessness

Weiner added the idea of controllability in 1979. This isn't a personality trait but rather involves whether the attributions relate to our own circumstances or to the circumstances of others. Those who attribute behaviour to something that they have control over would be said to use personal control, whilst those who make attributions that their behaviour is outside of their control have external control.

If we feel that things are out of our control then learned helplessness may occur. Learned helplessness (Seligman, 1975) occurs when an unpleasant or unwanted situation happens repeatedly and an individual is unable to find any escape from it. The individual eventually accepts the situation and thus develops learned helplessness. We may experience specific learned helplessness (linked to one particular situation) or global learned helplessness (linked to a group of situations).

Commentary

The problem with the addition of the controllability dimension is that it is difficult to see something as being both external and under your control and thus for external attributions, the notion of control does not seem to be very useful.

Weiner's model is a general model and whilst it can be applied to sport it is not specific to sport. Roberts and Pascuzzi (1979) and other researchers have found that in sport the four main attributions (ability, effort, luck and task difficulty) are not sufficient to categorize all possible attributions. Weiner did say that he had never intended these to be seen as the only four. Therefore, Roberts and Pascuzzi suggested that a more open-ended attribution system would allow athletes more flexibility when determining the reasons for their success or failure.

Measurement of attribution

The main way to measure attributions is in the form of a self-report scale – for example, the Causal Dimension Scale (CDS) developed by Russell (1982). The CDS consists of nine likert-scale items, three assessing each of the three main dimensions: stability, locus of causality and controllability. Extensive use of this scale led to the identification of problems with the controllability dimension, as it appeared to be simply measuring the same as locus of control. Therefore Russell et al (1992) revised the CDS. The CDS II comprises four rather than three dimensions: stability, locus of control, personal control and external control. These changes appeared to improve the reliability and validity of the measure.

An alternative measure of attributional style is the Sport Attributional Style Scale (SASS) developed by Hanrahan, Grove and Hattie (1989). This presents individuals with sixteen positive and negative sport events and requires them to state the cause of the event. These questions assess attribution across five dimensions: locus of control, stability and controllability, as on the CDS, with the addition of intentionality and globality. Again, research has found that this is also a reliable and valid measure.

Commentary

Although research has given support to both of the above self-report scales it is important to remember that any self-report scale relies on the honesty of the person completing it. It may also be influenced by subjective interpretation, as different words or phrases may mean different things to different people.

What factors can affect the attributions that we make?

Gender is one factor that greatly affects the attributions that we make. Females have lower expectations of success than males in most achievement situations. There are a number of possible reasons for this: genetic differences, socialization and others' expectations are just a few. Bird and Williams (1980) studied thirteen-year-old boys and girls and found that boys attributed success to their effort, whilst girls attributed success to luck.

One factor that can affect the way that individuals attribute behaviour, which can be more readily adjusted, is feedback from the teacher or coach.

Dweck (1978) carried out a study looking at teacher feedback and the effect that it had on performance. A group of junior school children were studied and the feedback that the teacher gave them was coded in two ways, firstly as positive or negative and secondly as about intellectual or non-intellectual aspects of their work. They found that boys received more negative feedback but mostly for non-intelligent aspects, such as neatness or conduct, whilst the negative feedback that the girls received was about their work. Boys' failure was attributed to lack of effort eight times more often than for girls.

Commentary

Coaches should be aware that their feedback affects how young players perceive their performance and too much negative feedback may lead to them dropping out of sport as they believe that they are 'no good at it'.

Errors in attribution

Individuals do tend to make errors when making attributions about behaviour. It is important to understand how these errors may occur and thus how it may be possible to alter the way that we make attributions. Self-serving bias is one type of error when individuals attribute success internally and failure externally. It is very rare to attribute success to external factors – for example, a rugby player attributing his team's success to the excellent refereeing. Gill (1980) asked women basketball players to give reasons for their successes and failures and found that overall they attributed success to their team doing well and failure to the other team's performance.

A second way that errors in attribution may occur is known as the actor–observer effect (Nisbett, 1973). The actor, the person doing the action, tends to attribute their behaviour to situational factors, thus seeing their behaviour as changeable. The observer, a person watching an individual's performance, tends to attribute the actor's behaviour to dispositional factors, therefore seeing his/her behaviour as fixed. For example, if Tim Henman misses a crucial shot, he might say that it was because the sun was in his eyes, whereas somebody watching might say that it was because he wasn't concentrating.

Cross-cultural research – attribution

The consequences of making incorrect attributions can be very severe and therefore it is vitally important to examine whether the attribution process is the same in all cultures. As sports teams are now made up of players from a range of cultures, and international competitions involve players from more countries than ever before, understanding attributions is becoming ever more important. It is very easy to attribute another player's behaviour to negative feeling when in actual fact it may be a behaviour that is common in their particular culture.

Research has shown that in many cases there are differences in the ways that different cultures make attributions. For example, Hau and Salili (1990) found that students from Hong Kong attributed factors such as effort, interest and ability as the most important causes of academic performance, regardless of success or failure, all of which are all internal attributions. Similarly, Moghaddam, Ditto and Taylor (1990) found that Indian women who had emigrated to Canada tended to attribute both successes and failures to internal causes.

Therefore, in connection with sport, it is possible that players from some cultures may attribute their failure to internal causes, whilst other team members may attribute it to bad luck. This will mean that some players feel that there is little that they can do to improve their performance, whilst others may shrug off failure believing that they will be luckier next time.

Commentary

There are drawbacks to the cross-cultural study of attributions, primarily concerned with the different interpretation of certain things. The perception of success and failure varies from culture to culture as does the meaning of luck and effort. Therefore it is difficult to be sure that words are interpreted in an identical way by all individuals, thus it is difficult to draw firm conclusions about the attribution process in different cultures.

Attribution retraining

If attributions are incorrect and are affecting sporting performance it is essential that players and coaches attempt to alter the attributions. Changing established attributions is known as attributional retraining (see Key Study 6).

KEY STUDY 6

Researcher: Dweck (1975)

Aim: To investigate the impact of attributional training on children's success.

Method: She looked at twelve children, aged 8–13, who had an extreme fear of failure but saw it as inevitable, an internal–stable attribution, and divided them into two groups. The children thought that they were taking part in a maths study to prevent any stigma about their failure. The first group experienced success each time they completed a task and the second group mostly experienced success, but when they failed the coach encouraged the child to attribute the failure to a lack of effort (unstable attribution) and thus something they could change (attributional retraining).

Results: When assessing the children's attributions afterwards it was found that those encouraged to change their attributions showed an improvement, whilst those who merely experienced success didn't.

Conclusions: This highlights the impact that incorrect attributions can have on an individual's belief in their own ability. It also illustrates how important it is that coaches ensure that appropriate attributions are being made. It highlights the fact that children are not motivated or rewarded simply by attaining success. They want to feel that they have some control over the situation and thus can accept some errors in the learning process.

The role of the coach in attribution retraining

Coaches need to observe the players and gain an insight into the attributions that they are making. One of the main ways to attempt to make a change in attributions is to encourage the players to view success as due to internal–stable factors and help them view any failure as being due to unstable, internal or external, factors. The players, with the coach's help can then begin to attribute behaviour appropriately (see RLA 13).

Real Life Application 13: Attribution training and achievement in sport

Thirty-five college beginner tennis players aged 17–21 were selected to take part in a study looking at the effects of attributional training. They were allocated to one of three conditions: controllable unstable condition (CU group), uncontrollable stable condition (US group) or no specific attributions condition (NA group). They met twice a week for five weeks, where they were given the Causal Dimension Scale II to complete and asked how well they expected to perform. They were completing two tasks, firstly they had to hit a target with the tennis ball and secondly they had to hit balls to the opposite area. The CU group were told that their performance was based on their effort and thus could be improved. The US group were told that their performance was based upon their innate ability and therefore some people would be better than others. The NA group just got general feedback. At the start of the study all attributed failure to uncontrollable, stable factors but by the end of the intervention the CU group had started to change their attributions to more functional ones. The US and NA groups did not experience this and the CU group also, by the end, believed they could be successful in the future.

Orbach, Singer and Price (1999).

Summary

- This study provides a clear example of how attributional training can have a definite effect on the way that players perceive their own success and failures.
- It is important for coaches to help players attribute their behaviour appropriately.

Questions

1 **a** Give an example of what an uncontrollable stable attribution would be.

b Give an example of a controllable unstable attribution.

2 Which type of attribution did RLA 13 suggest was best for players?

3 Why do you think that the CU group believed that they could be successful in the future?

Essay questions

1 Describe the four main types of attentional style and explain how each type may be useful in certain situations.

2 Discuss the potential benefits of utilizing imagery techniques in sporting situations.

3 How could an attributional retraining programme benefit children who believe that they are sports failures?

4 Social psychology and sport

This chapter focuses upon how individuals can be influenced by social factors in the first instance, to participate in sport. The chapter goes on to examine the effects other people can have on an individual's sporting performance by considering aggression, social facilitation, groups and leaders. Real Life Applications that are considered are:

- RLA 14: Aggression on the pitch
- RLA 15: Home is where the advantage is
- RLA 16: Marching altogether
- RLA 17: All in the same boat
- RLA 18: Sir Alex Ferguson
- RLA 19: Kevin Keegan resigns.

Why participate in sport?

The decision to participate in any sport is rarely based upon one single factor and as participation in childhood may set the scene for later life, it could be useful to have an understanding of what encourages some children to take part, whilst others avoid sporting situations. Whilst it is impossible to ignore a child's physiological make-up which obviously can have an impact on the type of sport that s/he may choose to take part in or avoid, it is not the only factor that influences participation. For example, every child who is tall is not going to become a high jumper, neither will every future high jumper be tall. Therefore we need to consider what other factors will influence a child's sporting participation.

There is a positive correlation between parental sporting ability and their children's sporting ability (see RLA 1, page 3). However, this alone cannot explain all participation, therefore we need to look at the effects of socialization. Socialization is the process of learning to live in and understand a culture by internalizing its beliefs, values, attitudes and social norms. Thus, sport socialization is simply learning to live in and understand a sport culture by internalizing its values, attitudes and norms. The people and institutions that socialize individuals into sport, via interactions, are known as socializing agents and these can be many and varied, including parents, siblings, peers, schools and the media.

Parents are obviously one of the first socializing agents in a child's life and research does suggest that they do have an impact on sports players' decisions to participate in the first place. For example, Sage (1980) found that after questioning hundreds of college athletes, over 90% said that parents had influenced their decision. There are different ways by which parents can socialize children into sport participation. One way is by encouraging them and reinforcing their participation, which leads to further participation. Another way, for parents who participate in sports, is providing a role model for their children, and consequently the children may imitate their parents.

Siblings may also have an effect on socializing children into sport participation in a similar way to parents. Research however suggests that the influence of siblings is not as great as the influence of parents.

Peers serve as a powerful socialization agent, as the desire to be accepted by friends, particularly during adolescence, is often overwhelming. Children and adolescents also place great value on sporting ability and thus the socialization effect of peers is great. As children become adolescents and start spending more time with their friends, the effect that peers can have becomes as prominent as the effect that parents can have in earlier years.

Schools can also act as a sport socialization agent due to the fact that they hold formal physical education classes and provide an opportunity for participation in sport at playtimes and lunchtimes. The impact that schools and teachers have can vary and is dependent upon other factors, such as the size of the school, the amount of participation and opportunities, out of school, for participation in sport. For many children, their experience of sport at school starts off a lifelong enjoyment of sport. However, for some children, their early experiences of sport at school can lead to avoidance of sporting activities for years to come.

As various forms of the media become ever more influential – for example, TV, newspapers and magazines – it is inevitable that they can act as a sport socialization agent. Children often see their heroes on TV or in the newspapers and try to emulate their behaviour. It is also possible that sports programmes and commentators can inadvertently encourage children to participate in sport.

Although children are subjected to so many socialization influences, they do still like to think that they chose to participate independently of other influences.

Sport as an influence on social development

Participation in sport can affect other areas of a child's development – for example, their social development. Children who are socialized into taking part in sporting activities are indirectly going to be learning social skills as well as sporting skills. The list below, although not exhaustive, provides some examples of skills that children may learn:

- how to co-operate with others
- the types of behaviour that are accepted by others
- how to behave in a group setting
- the importance of listening and paying attention
- the usefulness of observing role models to learn skills
- the idea of competition
- how to attribute their behaviour
- that different social settings require different types of behaviour.

Aggression

The mention of the word aggression linked to any sporting activity will provoke thoughts of a wide range of situations for most people – for example, unfair tackles in football, rugby players stamping on each other, or a boxer head-butting his opponent. The important question to consider in this chapter is when does 'fair' play end and aggression begin?

Many definitions of aggression have been put forward. For example, Dollard *et al* (1939) suggested that it is 'a sequence of behaviour in which the goal is to injure another person'. Along similar lines Berkowitz (1993) defined aggression as 'some kind of behaviour, that is carried out with the intention of harming someone'. Wann (1997) takes the definition of aggression a stage further stating that it is 'the intent to physically, verbally or psychologically

Aggressive behaviour during a football match

harm someone who is motivated to avoid such treatment and/or the physical destruction of property when motivated by anger'.

Commentary

The main difference between the first two definitions and the third one is that the final one considers a destructive act against an inanimate object to be aggression, whereas the other two don't. Thus, according to Wann's definition, a player who smashes his racquet – for example, Tim Henman in Wimbledon 2000 – would be considered aggressive, as it was an act that was motivated by anger.

Baron (1977) split aggressive behaviour into two main types:

• hostile
• instrumental.

In both, the intent is to harm another being or object. However, the reasons and reinforcement (see page 8) for each are different.

Firstly, with hostile aggression (also known as reactive aggression and angry aggression) the primary goal is the injury of another human being and the intention is to make the victim suffer. The reinforcement therefore is the pain and suffering that is caused. Hostile aggression is always accompanied by anger on the part of the aggressor. Biting off the ear of an opponent – for example, the 'Kevin Yates rugby incident' – would be an example of hostile aggression.

With instrumental aggression the intention is also to harm the victim but the reinforcement is not to observe the suffering but to receive some other type of reward – for example, winning or prestige. The aggressor sees the aggressive act as being instrumental in achieving their goal. An example of instrumental aggression would be 'hard men' midfield players in football who are willing to hurt the opposing players in order to achieve both status and winning scores – for example, Roy Keane.

A third type of behaviour linked closely to aggression is that of assertion. Assertiveness involves the legitimate physical or verbal force to achieve one's purpose. Assertive behaviour is not intended to harm the opposition but requires extra effort – and as there is no intent to harm, any resultant harm is incidental to the game. For example, even if an opposing footballer were injured during a tackle, providing the tackle was 'fair' this would be considered to be assertion.

Whilst it is quite simple to separate these different types of behaviour in theory, in practice there is always going to be some overlap. Who can say whether the extra force used in a tackle was fair or intended to hurt the other player?

Theories of aggression

There are numerous theories that have been put forward in attempts to explain why people are aggressive. These fall mainly into one of three categories:

• instinct
• frustration aggression
• social learning theories.

Here a number of traditional theories of aggression will be examined and applied to sport.

Instinct theory

The instinctual theories of aggression propose that humans possess an innate predisposition to be aggressive. These theories of aggression were popular at the start of the twentieth century and Freud was responsible for much of the work regarding the psychoanalytic aspect of instinct theory.

Freud believed that people are motivated towards self-destruction through the death instinct that he called Thanatos. He also believed that individuals have a life instinct called Eros. Thanatos and Eros are therefore in conflict and in order to resolve the conflict the self-destructive, aggressive energy needs to be turned outwards onto others.

Konrad Lorenz also believed that aggression was instinctive and he was responsible for much of the work on the ethological aspect of instinct theory. He proposed that humans and animals possess a fighting instinct that is triggered by certain environmental stimuli. For animals, displaying aggression to defend their territory is common; however, for humans this type of behaviour is less common. Lorenz believed that accumulated aggressive energy and the presence of aggression-releasing environmental stimuli would lead to the display of aggression.

Instinct theories support the notion of catharsis: the release of aggressive urges through aggression. This can be either real, the actual act of aggression, or symbolic, release through watching others be aggressive.

Both Freud and Lorenz believed that sport was very important due to its cathartic qualities. Although a number of psychologists and sports coaches support this view today, there has been a substantial amount of research that has refuted the notion that sport enables aggression catharsis. For example, Zillman, Johnson and Day (1974) compared the aggressive tendencies of athletes participating in aggressive sports, athletes participating in non-aggressive sports and non-athletes. The study found that there was no difference in aggressive tendencies between the three groups. This study contradicts the aggression catharsis theory as, according to this theory, those participating in aggressive sports would be expected to be less aggressive as they had the opportunity to release their aggression through sport, and the study that found this was not the case.

Commentary

The instincts that are crucial to these theories are very difficult to identify and measure and thus the theories are very difficult to test. The instinct theories could also be said to be reductionist as they focus only on innate explanations for aggression and ignore environmental factors. If aggression is innate then all cultures should be equally aggressive, but this is obviously not the case which therefore calls into question the usefulness of these theories.

Frustration–aggression hypothesis

Following the decline in popularity of the instinct theories, alternative explanations of aggression became more prominent. In the 1930s the drive reduction models of aggression became popular. These theories were initially quite closely linked to instinct theories. The main belief of these theories is that aggressive acts stem from an aggressive drive (drive is a state of inner tension) that is triggered by external stimuli. The most famous drive reduction theory was put forward by Dollard, Miller, Doob, Mourer and Sears (1939) – the frustration aggression hypothesis. This proposed that the inability to attain a goal leads to frustration. The frustration triggers an aggressive drive that leads to aggression.

Commentary

Dollard et al's theory has been criticized for being over simplistic as they suggested that a blocked goal would always lead to frustration and frustration would always lead to aggression. Unlike the instinct theories they are not claiming that aggression is either innate or learnt, rather they suggested that it could be innate or learnt or a combination of both. In common with the instinct theories there is also the belief in the cathartic effects of sport, as once the aggression has been released they believe that the frustration will have diminished and thus further aggression would be unlikely.

Berkowitz (1989) reformulated the frustration aggression hypothesis and proposed that frustration results from an inability to attain a goal, creating a 'readiness' for aggression. This frustration is more likely to lead to aggression if aggressive cues (objects or persons currently or previously associated with aggression) are present. Although Berkowitz does say that aggressive cues do not have to be present to lead to overt aggression they do make it more likely. He thought that sport might sometimes have a cathartic effect; however this would be reduced if the frustration continued, aggressive behaviour becomes learnt or the aggression leads to anxiety, which will in turn lead to further frustration.

Commentary

The validity of the frustration aggression hypothesis has been increased with Berkowitz's amendments. Saying that frustration is likely to lead to aggression, but that it doesn't always happen, and introducing the idea of aggressive cues, leads to it being a more useful framework with which to assess aggression in sport.

Social learning theory

The third main approach to explain human aggression is via social learning theory, proposed by Bandura (1973). This theory suggests that aggression is learnt through operant conditioning and observational learning (see Chapter 1, pages 7–10). Whilst Bandura acknowledges the importance of operant conditioning (behaviour that is reinforced is more likely to be repeated – for example, a football player being cheered by the fans for aggressive tackles) he believes that observational learning is more important.

Commentary

Bandura's proposals that aggression is learnt and that viewing aggression leads to further aggression, oppose the notion of catharsis. Research has shown that younger players do seem to model themselves on older players and thus it seems reasonable that aggression could be learnt as part of this observational learning.

Does aggression affect sporting performance or not?

There is little research actually looking at how aggression influences performance and thus it is difficult to draw any conclusions.

Silva (1979) did a controlled study looking at aggression and performance. Confederates provoked hostile aggression in individuals taking part in competitive pegboard and three-person basketball. It was found that those provoked into hostile aggression exhibited less concentration and poorer performance than non-provoked individuals in the same conditions.

This led Silva to suggest that aggression tends to inhibit rather than enhance sporting performance, for two reasons: the shift of attention from performance and the fact that a player's arousal level may go past the optimum arousal level for performance.

However, not all research supports this. Russell (1974) concluded that a positive correlation exists between the number of successful goals and assists, in ice hockey, and the amount of hostile aggression.

Commentary

There could be considered to be a problem of measurement with the ice hockey studies as hostile aggression was taken to be the penalties awarded and the challenges to authority – these might have been no more than assertion.

Based on the amount of current research it is not completely clear how aggression affects performance in sport.

Situational factors and their effects on aggression

If an individual player is aggressive, can we expect to see that aggression every time s/he participates in sport or could other situational factors have an effect? Research has been carried out into various situational factors and some of the factors will be considered below.

Temperature

General psychological research has found that temperature can affect behaviour, with the suggestion that the higher the temperature, the more aggressive people are. A study by Reifman, Larrick and Fein (1991) used data from more than 800 baseball games played in 1986, 1987 and 1988 and found that there was a relationship between the number of aggressive acts and the increase in temperature, thus demonstrating a linear relationship. In laboratory experiments the relationship between heat and aggression has been found to be curvilinear – aggression increases up to an optimum point beyond which further increases in temperature lead to a decline in aggression.

Commentary

The likely reason for these differences is that in the lab setting, individuals will begin to focus their attention on escaping rather than on aggression, whilst in the field settings escape is unlikely and thus aggression continues to rise. Therefore in sport, it is likely that increases in temperature will lead to increases in aggression, as players will not easily be able to escape the heat.

Point differential

Other factors more directly related to the game may also affect aggressive behaviour. For example, when teams are very close in points there is little aggressive behaviour; more aggression is displayed as the point differential increases. Russell (1983) found, when examining 430 hockey games, that there was more aggression if three goals or more separated the teams than if the scores were close.

Location

The location of the game can also affect the amount of aggression with away teams tending to demonstrate more aggression. This may link into the idea of home field advantage (see page 51).

League position

If the frustration aggression hypothesis is correct, teams at the top of the league would be expected to be less aggressive, as they are achieving their goal and thus should not be experiencing frustration. Conversely, teams in lower positions should be frustrated by their league position and demonstrate more aggressive behaviour. Russell and Drewery (1976) found that this pattern appeared to be true, with the team that was first in the league, demonstrating the least aggression. However, they found that as teams moved up through the league, they exhibited greater levels of aggression as the frustration of not being in first position became more salient. Other researchers have disagreed with this finding, suggesting that the team in bottom place is more aggressive.

Commentary

Although there seems to be general agreement that the team in first place is least aggressive, further research is needed to investigate the pattern of aggression amongst the other teams.

Spectator aggression

Researchers have found no difference in the trait aggressiveness of sport fans and non-fans and thus sport spectators do not necessarily arrive at events feeling aggressive. The important question that psychologists have been attempting to answer is what leads to spectator aggression?

Applying the theories that were examined earlier may shed some light on the situation. Instinct theorists argue that sport is a safe way for spectators to release their aggression. However, if this cathartic effect were to be true then the release through viewing the aggression would lead to a reduction in aggression. This does not seem to be the case – researchers have found across a wide variety of sports that viewing sports players acting aggressively leads to increases in spectator aggression. For example, a study carried out by Goldstein and Arms (1971) compared spectators' hostility, using a questionnaire at two sporting events – firstly, an Army–Navy football game and secondly a gymnastics competition between the Army and Temple University. Spectators were tested both pre-game and post-game and the researchers found no difference in hostility levels for the spectators at the gymnastic meet. However, there was greater hostility after watching the football game.

Frustration aggression theories would suggest that spectators of the losing team would be more aggressive as their goal (winning) was being blocked. Much research has been carried out in this field and has supported this suggestion. Social learning theory would suggest that spectators would behave more aggressively after watching an aggressive sports match as they are learning through observation. Russell (1981) carried out a study that demonstrated that this appeared to be the case. Two ice hockey games were examined to assess the link between aggression and spectator aggression. Game 1 was violent, there were 142 minutes of assessed penalties, whilst game 2 was well played, with only 46 minutes of assessed penalties. A Mood Adjective Checklist (which measures aggression and arousal) was given to randomly selected spectators at predetermined times in both games. They found an increase in arousal and aggressive feelings as aggression increased on the field.

RLA 14 illustrates the effect that aggression at sporting events can have on spectators and how they, in turn, can influence the event.

Real Life Application 14:

Aggression on the pitch

Celtic 0 – 2 Rangers
5 June 1946
Victory Cup semi-final replay

This has to go down as one of the most sensational clashes of all time. Two Celtic players were sent off, a spectator armed with a bottle attacked the referee, police fought with spectators on the pitch and the terraces were awash with fighting. The spark had come when Rangers, already a goal up, won a penalty, prompting mass Celtic protests. George Young went to take the penalty but was prevented by Celtic players, which resulted in Celtic's George Paterson being sent off. The penalty was eventually taken and Young scored. Before the game could restart, a spectator ran onto the pitch with a bottle and aimed several blows at the referee. Other fans were now on the pitch trying to encourage the Celtic players to leave the pitch. The police arrived and riots broke out on the terraces.

Adapted from *FourFourTwo*, January 2000.

Summary

- The above description of a violent football match is an example of how aggression by players can influence spectators and vice versa.

Questions

1 How would a social learning theorist explain the aggression in the game?

2 How could the aggression be explained using the frustration aggression theory?

3 What factors are there about this game that could have led to increased aggression?

Reducing aggression in sport

As aggression becomes ever more evident amongst players and spectators – for example, the violence between opposing fans in the UEFA 2000 cup final between Arsenal and Galatasary – it is becoming increasingly necessary to try to find ways of reducing aggression. Unfortunately, some people do not actively discourage violence and aggression and therefore as children are watching their heroes receive status, money and adulation for their sporting prowess, including aggressive behaviour, they are aiming to emulate them.

It is possible to reduce levels of aggression connected with sport if everyone involved is committed to it. Many of the suggestions from the research link in with the learning theories that were examined in Chapter 1. These include providing young sports players with non-aggressive models and the use of reward for controlling tempers in a volatile situation and punishment or negative reinforcement for aggressive acts. There is a commitment in international sporting events to reduce aggression as teams are now being rewarded for 'fair play'. For example, the football World Cup awards a Fair Play title to the team with the least number of bookings.

Coaches should ensure that they deal with aggression appropriately during training and help their players to develop coping strategies for dealing with situations that may otherwise lead to aggression (see Key Study 7).

Reducing aggression by the fans is potentially more difficult. However, suggestions have been made following research. These include reducing the media portrayal of hatred between opposing fans and actively discouraging acts of aggression. Again, by using reinforcement and punishment, fans' behaviour could be shaped to be more appropriate.

KEY STUDY 7

Researchers: Brunelle, Janelle and Tennant (1999)

Aim: To examine the most effective way of reducing aggression in footballers.

Method: They used 57 male footballers aged between 18 and 28. They measured their anger scores before carrying out the study and found that they were all quite similar. The participants were randomly assigned to one of three conditions: role-playing, anger awareness or a control group. The first two groups both had the same short educational lecture during their hour session each week. The role-play group were then given a live demonstration of alternative responses to anger feelings and they acted them out. The anger awareness group followed the lecture by discussing their anger and they kept journals of their feelings of anger. The control group spent the same amount of time together as the other two but anger control was not mentioned. They focused on learning techniques such as relaxation.

Results: Following the intervention programme, the participants' anger was measured, using observation, a checklist and self-report measures, over 15 matches. It was found that those who had been in the role-play group demonstrated less aggression and anger, followed by the anger awareness group.

Conclusions: The finding that the role play method was the most useful in reducing anger and aggression obviously lends support to the social learning theory's belief in the importance of modelling. This therefore could prove to be very useful for coaches.

Social facilitation

Social facilitation is concerned with the effect that other people may have on our sporting performance. Do sports players behave any differently when they are being watched or appraised, or is performance relatively stable? The important question to address here is whether the presence of others will impair or enhance sporting performance.

There are two main ways in which we perform in the presence of others. Firstly, working alongside people, which is known as the co-action effect – for example, members of a football team playing together, or doubles players in tennis matches. Secondly, performing with people watching us, which is known as the audience effect – for example, playing in a competition in front of a large crowd of fans, or performing a newly learnt skill in front of family or friends. There are also different types of audience: inactive and reactive. Inactive spectators are simply passive observers who do not interact with the sportsperson – for example, audiences at snooker or bowls championships. Reactive audiences respond to the sportsperson's behaviour – for example, spectators at football or rugby matches.

The early work looking at the effects of the presence of others on performance was carried out at the turn of the twentieth century. Triplett (1898) looked at competitive cycling records and noted that paced times were 35 seconds per mile faster than unpaced times and competitive times were even faster. This was followed up by a controlled study looking at children winding fishing reels. He found that they wound them faster in pairs than when alone.

Allport (1920) continued to investigate the effects others have on performance and asked college students to complete multiplication sums at the same time as others but they were instructed not to compete. It was found that students completed more when working with others than when they were alone. Other researchers – for example, Clayton (1978) – have even found a similar effect occurring in animals when in the presence of other animals. It has been found that chickens eat more in front of other chickens and ants displayed more nest-building activity when working with other ants.

Social facilitation and performance

Drive theory

In an attempt to help to explain the effects others can have on performance, Zajonc (1965) proposed the Drive Theory of Social Facilitation and explained two types of effect. This links in with drive theory of arousal (see Chapter 2). The suggestion of this theory is that as a skill becomes well learned it requires less arousal to be performed and the presence of others stimulates arousal, thus both can affect performance.

Thus drive theory would suggest that, firstly, the presence of others when carrying out a simple or well-learned task would actually improve performance and secondly, for complex or novel tasks, the presence of others may damage performance.

In summary, Zajonc drew four conclusions from this theory:

- the presence of others leads to arousal or 'drive'
- increased arousal leads to an increased chance that the dominant response will occur
- for simple or well-learned tasks the dominant response is appropriate and leads to improved performance
- for complex tasks the dominant response will be incorrect due to over-arousal and will thus lead to a decline in performance.

Critics of the drive theory argue that these effects do not always occur, and therefore look to other theories, particularly the inverted U theory (see Chapter 2 for more details).

Inverted U theory

According to the inverted U theory, the presence of others may enhance performance but only up to a point, beyond which performance will show a steady decline. This theory also proposes that the optimum level of performance is dependent upon the sport, the skill level and the individual and thus the presence of others will not have same effect on every individual or in every situation.

Alternative explanations of social facilitation

Cottrell's evaluation–apprehension theory

Zajonc had proposed that the mere presence of others was sufficient to elicit arousal, which in turn would affect performance. However, Cottrell (1968) suggested that it isn't the presence of others that leads to arousal, but the apprehension of being evaluated by others, which he believed is a type of social anxiety. He thus developed his evaluation apprehension theory. This idea stems from the fact that being watched doesn't always lead to an impairment of performance.

According to Cottrell, you might expect a sportsperson to perform well when being watched by his/her family, as s/he is relaxed and not fearful of being evaluated. However, if being watched by a panel of judges, evaluation would be expected and thus performance may decline.

Commentary

Whilst this theory does seem to put forward a valuable argument and a reasonable explanation for how the presence of others may affect performance, it must be remembered that the effects it suggests do not always occur. Think back to when you were younger and were playing sport while being watched by your proud family – did you always perform well? Probably not, as, although you may not have feared them evaluating your performance, you may have wanted to do well to 'please' them and thus put yourself under greater pressure, leading to over-arousal.

Baron's distraction–conflict theory

Baron (1986) also incorporated cognitive factors into his explanation of social facilitation. He devel-

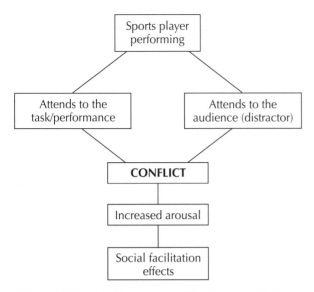

Figure 4.1: Baron's distraction–conflict theory applied to sport

oped the distraction–conflict theory in which he linked the amount of attention needed to perform tasks and the amount required to attend to an audience. His suggestion was that it is this conflict that affects performance. Figure 4.1 shows how this would apply in sport.

Therefore we can see that the spectators may provide a distraction, which leads to a conflict with the attention required to complete the task, which leads to arousal, which may in turn affect the individual's performance.

Commentary

Whilst all of the above theories have some drawbacks and no single theory can explain all aspects of the effects that the presence of others has on our performance, including the reasons for these effects, all have something useful to offer to assist in explaining the phenomena. Therefore, it is now more accepted to attempt to integrate the ideas, as Chapman (1974) proposed, in an attempt to explain social facilitation effects. Chapman suggested that the mere presence of an audience would have more effect on performance than no audience, and an audience that is able to evaluate sports players' performance will have a greater effect than a merely present audience will. As the audience become more able to evaluate performance they presumably will also become more distracting and therefore will have an even greater impact on performance. Research has supported Chapman's suggestions.

Audience effects and sport performance

The research directly related to sport has been gen-

erally inconclusive. However, one finding that has been supported is that of home field advantage. Put simply, this is the fact that sports teams perform better when they are playing on their 'home' ground. Schwartz and Barsky (1977) gathered statistical information on 1880 major league baseball games, 1092 football games, 542 ice hockey league games and 1485 basketball games. They found that the home team won 53% of games in baseball, 60% in football and 64% in basketball and ice hockey. Leonard (1989) reported that the host nation wins more medals in the Olympics than they have done before or since. This finding has been supported by Australia's excellent performance in the Sydney 2000 summer Olympics.

Courneya and Carron (1992) carried out an extensive review of the home field advantage literature and confirmed that it is a real and measurable phenomenon. The greatest home field advantage appeared to be for football, hockey and basketball with the least advantage for baseball.

Bray (1999) reviewed the literature on home field advantage to look at a more specific aspect of it. Previous research into the phenomena had focused on an overall performance in a particular sporting league, but this does not allow the identification of the extent of the home field advantage for individual teams. Bray reviewed data from 20 seasons of ice hockey, covering more than 30,000 games. He measured home winning as an individual team's home win percentage minus their away win percentage. Using this measurement he found that teams won on average 17.3 % more games at home than away.

Commentary

Bray's study allows the examination of weaker teams who have not won many games. If a team has only won 5 games out of 50 in a season, but all of these have been

Fans supporting their team

at home, it still provides strong evidence for the existence of a home field advantage. Thus the more important question might be why teams win more often at home.

Why does the home field advantage occur?

As the existence of the home field advantage phenomenon is generally accepted (see RLA 15 for a further example), attention has now turned to attempts to explain why it occurs. There seem to be several possible reasons.

The main suggestion as to why this occurs is due to the effects of a supportive home audience. A number of points are linked to this. Firstly, the amount of noise that the audience makes – the greater the noise, the greater the impression of support. Secondly, the number of people actually in the stadium – there is a positive correlation between crowd density (the number of fans present related to the size of the stadium) and the team performance (Pollard, 1986). The number of fans alone is not a major factor, the crowd density is more important.

It is also possible that non-audience effects influence the home field advantage. These include the home team engaging in more assertive play. For example, Varca (1980) looked at the home field advantage in basketball and found that the home team demonstrated more functionally aggressive behaviour (blocked shots etc.) whilst the away team demonstrated more dysfunctionally aggressive behaviour (fouls). Other possible influences are the home team's familiarity with the stadium and the fact that the home team does not have to travel to the fixture.

Commentary

It is important to appreciate that it is likely to be a combination of factors that lead to the home field advantage and obviously it is very difficult to study some of them in isolation. Arguably, the greatest influence is the effect of the audience, although this would not be appropriate for all sports and is most relevant to sports that have reactive or interactive audiences.

Real Life Application 15:

Home is where the advantage is

In the football World Cup teams tend to do better when they are the host team.

Year	Host	Host team position
1930	Uruguay	Winner
1934	Italy	Winner
1938	France	Quarter finalists
1950	Brazil	Runners-up
1954	Switzerland	Quarter finalists
1958	Sweden	Runners-up
1962	Chile	Semi-finalists
1966	England	Winner
1970	Mexico	Quarter-finalists
1974	West Germany	Winner
1978	Argentina	Winner
1982	Spain	Second round
1986	Mexico	Quarter-finalists
1990	Italy	Semi-finalists
1994	USA	Second round
1998	France	Winner

Adapted from *The Independent,* 11 June 1998.

Summary

• The above table illustrates that the host team generally does well in the World Cup and in many cases their performance when they were the host team was better than they had achieved before or have achieved since.

Questions

1 What percentage of the host teams have reached at least the semi-final stage of the World Cup?

2 What type of advantage may be one explanation for this success?

3 Suggest three different factors that could explain why this type of advantage occurred.

Implications of audience effects for coaches

In light of the findings as to how audiences influence performance there are ways that coaches could use this information to help sports players.

• When players are learning new skills do not let people watch as the players' fear of evaluation may be too great, leading to a poor performance.
• To maximize the co-action effect it could be useful for teams to train together to enhance performance.

- Coaches could teach the players strategies to minimize the effects of distraction (see Chapter 3 on attentional style, page 32).

The effect of performers on others

Whilst the majority of the research has focused on how audiences can affect the performers' behaviour, it is also worth noting that players can affect the audience. Bad behaviour from a player can lead to hostile reactions from the audience, which may then in turn affect the performance. When David Beckham returned to football after being sent off for kicking an Argentinean player, Diego Simeone, in the 1998 World Cup, the reaction from fans was very hostile which had an effect on his club team's performance and morale.

The wider-reaching effects of individual player's behaviour should also be considered. Taking the above example, young fans who idolize David Beckham will see his behaviour and believe that it is acceptable and copy it, thus demonstrating 'modelling' effects. This links in with the idea of vicarious reinforcement. Young fans see a player – for example, Dennis Wise – getting respect from others for aggressive behaviour and this leads to the fans feeling good as they are copying him.

Good role models can obviously have a good effect on the audience and on individual fans and thus players like Gary Lineker should be put forward to young players in an attempt to get them to emulate his behaviour.

Groups and leaders

Many sports are played in teams and the individuals within that team are dependent upon each other for success. This section therefore aims to answer the question of what constitutes a group and how can group (team) behaviour affect sporting performance.

McGrath (1984) defines a group as 'those social aggregates that involve mutual awareness and potential interaction'. Therefore, a collection of individuals does not make a group. There needs to be a number of defining features, which include:

- interaction between members
- some positive feelings towards each other
- a collective identity – seeing themselves as a unit, distinct from other groups (which may include an assumption of particular values or ways of behaving)
- a sense of shared purpose – members need to interact and depend upon each other to achieve objectives.

Group structure

As we can see from the description above, a team is more than a collection of players, and in order for the group to function effectively it is necessary for a structure to develop within the group. Members take on certain roles (sets of behaviours expected of a person in a certain position) either formally or informally.

- **Formal roles** are those that are part of the structure of the group – for example, a defender or a striker. There are also other types of formal roles such as Captain or Coach.
- **Informal roles** are not part of the group structure but they help the group to function – for example, individual players may be seen as a mediator or a mentor to new members. Informal roles may also be negative – for example, one group member may be the main troublemaker.

Roles are very important to the functioning of a team, because if they are developed appropriately they should allow the team to be more effective. This is partly due to the fact that it should enable players to have an overall picture of the team and thus be aware of how their contribution fits in. Therefore, players who have roles tend to put in more effort and be more committed.

How do groups form?

Initially a new team will be no more than a collection of individuals, however Tuckman (1965) suggested a group goes through four stages whilst developing.

1 Forming – at the first stage team members are getting to know each other and begin to test relationships with others in the group.
2 Storming – conflict starts to arise between team members, with rebellion against the leader, as members are trying to establish their roles.
3 Norming – co-operation begins to replace conflict and members start working towards common goals. Group cohesion is beginning to develop.
4 Performing – this occurs once the relationships have stabilized and the primary goal for all is success.

Group cohesion

As the team moves through the stages described

above, members are establishing their group norms: what their beliefs are, behaviours that are appropriate or inappropriate and how they are going to achieve their aims. Once established, members show their commitment to the team by following the group norms. Members who deliberately flout these norms are preventing the team from performing as cohesively as it otherwise could. Part of the leader of the group's role is to try to ensure that the norms are maintained. The following of the group norms leads to the team becoming a cohesive unit, whereby the whole group is united in its efforts.

Is a highly cohesive team more likely to be successful?

Firstly, we need to consider the two types of cohesion:

- task
- social.

Task cohesion is the extent to which members of the group are committed to working together to achieve their goal, usually winning a game. Social cohesion is concerned with the amount that the group members actually like each other and offer support and trust to one another. It is possible to have one type of cohesion without the other – for example, as an individual you might be very committed to winning but not really like the other people in the team.

There are a number of external factors that may affect the level of group cohesion and the effect that this has on sporting performance. One of the main factors is obviously the sport that is involved. In interactive sports, where the members need to interact to be successful, such as football, netball and volleyball, high levels of group cohesion seems to enhance performance (see RLA 16). However, in coactive sports where members of a team do not need to directly interact, such as golf, bowling and athletics, the level of group cohesion does not appear to affect performance.

Personal characteristics of group members may also affect cohesion. Teams where members are similar in age and ability tend to have greater cohesion than those with a very diverse membership. Small teams also tend to be more cohesive, as there is more identifiable responsibility on each player.

Real Life Application 16: Marching altogether

Leeds United football team celebrating goal

Michael Bridges loves playing for Leeds United. Two years before he started playing for the team he knew that they would be a side that he would really put his heart into because there was so much enthusiasm from existing team members. He believes that their strength is the fact that they attack well. However, that alone cannot explain their success. Michael acknowledges that they do have a strong back four and a solid midfield, making them a strong team all round. The forwards and the midfield really appreciate the defence because they know that if they are not scoring goals, their defence will not be conceding any goals either.

Adapted from *FourFourTwo*, April 2000.

Summary

- Michael Bridges is talking about what it feels like to be part of a successful team.
- Part of this success is obviously due to the clear cohesion that exists.

Questions

1 What evidence is there in the article that team members have clearly defined roles?

2 Why is it difficult to say whether Leeds United is successful due to team cohesion?

3 What characteristics would you advise Leeds United's manager to look for in future signings to ensure they fit into the team?

Measurement of team cohesion

One of the earliest measures of team cohesion was the Sports Cohesiveness Questionnaire (SCQ) devised by Martens and Peterson (1971). Most of the questions, however, focused on social cohesion and despite its initial popularity there was little research to support it as a valid measure. Other measures were developed, moving more towards a multidimensional approach, and in 1985 Widmeyer, Brawley and Carron devised a self-report questionnaire – Group Environment Questionnaire (GEQ) to measure four dimensions of group cohesion:

- group integration – task
- group integration – social
- individual attractions in the group – task
- individual attractions in the group – social.

This measure included eighteen likert-scale items that measured the above four dimensions. A number of research studies have found the GEQ to have strong reliability and validity.

This therefore acknowledges the multidimensional nature of group cohesion and thus may enable the identification of specific areas for improvement.

Commentary

Once again the main method of measuring team cohesion is the use of self-report scales. Whilst research has shown that some measures have good reliability and validity, it must be remembered that the responses to any self-report scale are open to subjective interpretation.

Group cohesion and performance

In order to assess the value of encouraging group cohesion, the effect upon performance needs to be investigated. Numerous studies have found a significant, positive relationship between measures of team cohesion and performance in interactive sports.

Commentary

The main drawback with studies in this area is ascertaining the direction of causality. Are the teams performing well because their levels of cohesion are high, or is their level of cohesion high because they are performing well?

The effects of winning or losing

A study that made an attempt to investigate the effects of winning or losing on perceived group cohesion was carried out by Kozub and Button (2000). Sixty male rugby players and sixty male swimmers completed the GEQ immediately before and after rugby matches and dual swim meets. They found that only the two task dimensions of the GEQ altered significantly from pre to post competition. For rugby, the group's task integration mean score increased slightly following a win but decreased significantly following a loss. For swimmers, the mean score for group task integration increased significantly from pre to post meet for both winners and losers. For both sports, the attractions to the group task increased from pre to post event regardless of the outcome.

Commentary

This research suggests that different dimensions of group cohesion, according to Widmeyer, Brawley and Carron's GEQ, may be affected differently by success and failure. It does appear that the perceived level of cohesion does increase following success in some sports.

The drawback of this study is that only two sports have been examined and only male participants have been used. Therefore, in order to investigate the links between group cohesion and performance further, a wider range of sports and participants of both sexes would be needed.

Group performance

How does being a member of a group affect performance? Is it simply the sum of all the individual team members' performances or do other factors appear to have an effect?

Steiner's model of group performance

Steiner (1972) proposed a model to clarify the individual/group relationship in sport, which can be expressed as:

actual productivity = potential productivity – losses due to faulty group processes

Potential productivity is the group's best possible performance given its resources and the task demands. Faulty processes can be split into two main areas: co-ordination losses and motivational losses. Firstly, co-ordination losses are due to problems of co-ordination and timing and to prevent these losses, coaches should allow more time for practising timing and the pattern of player's movements. Secondly, motivational losses occur when the level of motivation differs for individuals within a group.

Group size and performance

The Ringelmann effect

Ringelmann, at the turn of the twentieth century, looked at individuals' and groups' performance on a rope-pulling exercise. He found that the groups did not pull with the amount of force you would expect by adding up the individual scores.

He found that when two people were pulling the rope their effort equalled 93% of the average of the individuals' performance, 85% of the individuals' performance when three people were pulling and the performance slipped to only 49% when eight people were pulling.

Ingham *et al* (1974) replicated Ringelmann's study and found similar results up to a point. However, they found that for groups larger than three there was no notable further decrease in performance. They also took the study a step further to look at whether the decrease was due to co-ordination or motivational losses, as Steiner had proposed. They concluded that decreases were due to motivational losses. This reduction in individual effort that occurs when people are working collectively is known as 'social loafing'.

Latane also looked at group performance and concluded that it decreased the larger the group. In their first study, Latane *et al* (1979) asked groups of differing numbers to clap and shout. They con-

Rope-pulling task – are all individuals putting in maximum effort?

firmed the Ringelmann effect, finding that by the time six people were involved the effort was only 40% of the average individual effort, clearly showing the effects of social loafing. Latane *et al* carried out a second study that attempted to identify the type of losses that were occurring in the group performance. They used actual groups, who could see other members of the group, and pseudo-groups who were supposedly connected up to other group members via earphones. Despite the instructions and background noise in the earphones individuals were actually alone. They found that for the actual groups the performance was lower than for the pseudo-groups but even the pseudo-groups, when believing there were six members in the group, only managed 74% of the average individual effort. As the co-ordination losses had been eliminated in the pseudo-groups it is possible to conclude that the loss in performance was due to motivational factors.

Further investigations looked at the causes of social loafing and below are some of the possible reasons.

- Thinking others are not committed and not wanting to be 'used' by the others.
- Thinking others will cover up for lack of effort.
- Thinking individual effort will make little difference.
- Thinking individual efforts can't be identified.

Commentary

Interestingly, if performance is being directly monitored, effort increases. Therefore, this seems to suggest that in order to prevent social loafing it is essential that it is possible to easily identify each individual's effort.

Cross-cultural research – group performance

Research suggests that social loafing is not a universal phenomenon. Whilst studies that have been carried out in the West have shown a clear pattern that individual's productivity in a group is not as great as their productivity when alone, this is not found in all cultures. For example, Earley (1989) demonstrated that when management trainees from the United States and China were compared on group performances, social loafing only occurred in the American participants. Other studies have actually shown that not only does social loafing not occur, an opposite effect can be seen (individual performance is enhanced by being in a group) which has been termed 'social striving'.

One explanation for the occurrence of social striving is the fact that certain cultures, such as the Chinese and Japanese cultures, foster interpersonal interdependence and thus value group collective functioning very highly. As a result, groups in these cultures tend to be more productive than the individuals would be if performing alone.

In a sport setting, social striving would lead to a team being highly motivated and efficient and their productivity would be greater than the sum of their individual efforts. Although this phenomenon has been found to occur more in cultures that greatly value group performances, there are occasions when it has been seen in Western cultures, see RLA 17 for an example.

Real Life Application 17:
All in the same boat

Olympics 2000: the gold medal-winning British coxless four rowing team

Steve Redgrave and Matthew Pinsent have paid tribute to their rowing partners, Tim Foster and James Cracknell, who complete the British coxless four team that is aiming to make Olympic history. Redgrave and Pinsent are quick to praise Foster and Cracknell, who hardly share the limelight, as the four have produced a unit that has worked very well together over the last four years.

Pinsent explains how their success is certainly not down to Steve and himself with the others 'tacked on', rather, every member of the group relies on the others to perform. Redgrave also refers to the excellent team spirit and believes that the very strong relationship that they all have is due to the underlying factor that they are aiming for the same thing and they all need each other to achieve that thing.

Adapted from an article on www.bbc.co.uk/sport, 26 August 2000.

Summary

- The British coxless four rowing team demonstrate that the phenomena of social loafing does not always occur when individuals work together in a team aiming for the same goal.

Questions

1 What do you think the 'thing' that all the team members are striving for is?

2 Do you think that the coxless four rowing team could be an example of the phenomenon of 'social striving'? Give reasons for your answer.

Leadership

Having seen how groups develop and perform it is also important to investigate how leaders develop and how their role can further influence sporting performance.

Barrow (1977) described leadership as 'the behavioural process influencing individuals and groups towards set goals'.

What makes an effective leader?

There are many characteristics that can influence how effective a leader is and the following are probably four of the most important. An effective leader needs to have:

- good communication skills
- high motivation and enthusiasm
- a clear vision of what needs to be achieved
- the ability to empathize.

Leadership style

Although certain characteristics can be identified as important for a leader to possess, the way in which s/he uses them can vary. Thus there are a number of different leadership styles and Lewin, Lippitt and White (1939) identified three of these (see Table 4.1).

They suggested that each style could be useful in certain circumstances and the ability to switch between them is important. The style of leadership can affect group performance – for example, if the leader is absent and the team have to continue without him/her, teams who have an authoritarian leader will do very little and will probably become

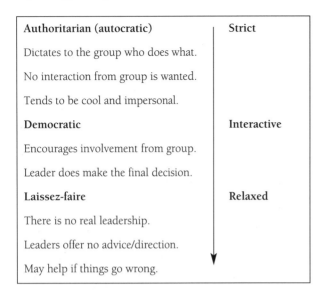

Authoritarian (autocratic)	Strict
Dictates to the group who does what.	
No interaction from group is wanted.	
Tends to be cool and impersonal.	
Democratic	Interactive
Encourages involvement from group.	
Leader does make the final decision.	
Laissez-faire	Relaxed
There is no real leadership.	
Leaders offer no advice/direction.	
May help if things go wrong.	

Table 4.1: Leadership styles

aggressive with each other. Those teams with a democratic leader will continue with their tasks in an appropriate manner, whilst those teams with a leader who adopts the laissez-faire style will give up and do nothing.

Other factors are important and researchers have identified two categories of leadership behaviour:

- task-orientated – deciding team priorities, identifying weaknesses and keeping individuals 'on task'
- person-orientated – having a high level of communication and rapport with others and showing and gaining consideration, trust and respect.

An interaction of the two is the most beneficial.

Is a leader born or made?

Is it possible to identify leaders at birth or do their leadership qualities develop over time? This raises the nature–nurture debate. There are two ways to investigate this: by looking at the personal qualities (traits) of leaders, or by looking at the way leaders behave in certain circumstances.

Great man theory (trait approach)

This theory suggested that successful leaders have similar traits (intelligence, assertiveness, ambition, they are dominant and they are usually male) thus supporting the viewpoint that leaders are born. This would therefore support the notion of leadership qualities being due to nature not nurture.

Commentary

Such a narrow focus has led to criticisms and thus poten-tial problems with the great man theory as it ignored situational factors and interactions with others.

Researchers therefore started to look at what behaviours were associated with successful leaders.

Fiedler's contingency model of leadership

Fiedler (1967) classified leaders as either task-orientated (focused on performance) or relationship-orientated (focused on personal relationships). This was done by measuring the leader's attitude towards the person they found most difficult to work with (the least preferred co-worker, or LPC). Leaders who saw LPC in a fairly positive way were classed as relationship-orientated whilst leaders who saw LPC in a negative way were classed as task-orientated.

According to Fiedler, the different styles could be appropriate at different times. Partially it depends upon the situational favourableness. A favourable situation is one where there is a warm positive relationship between the leader and group members, there is a clear task structure and the leader is considered to be strong.

- Task-orientated leaders are most effective in both the most and least favourable situations.
- Relationship-orientated leaders are most effective in moderately favourable situations.

Commentary

There are a number of problems with the model proposed by Fiedler and these include the fact that subsequent research findings to test the model are inconclusive, possibly due to the fact that the variables are difficult to assess. Some researchers question the appropriateness of the model for specific sports. A further drawback is that the classification of the leader is based on results from self-report questionnaire and thus is subjective.

Chelladurai's multidimensional model

According to Chelladurai (1984, 1990) there are five types of leadership behaviour:

1 training and instruction – behaviour that is aimed at improving performance
2 democratic – allows decisions to be made collectively
3 autocratic – gives the leader personal authority
4 social support – concern for the well-being of others
5 rewarding – provides team members with positive reinforcement.

These behaviours can be measured using the Leadership Scale for Sport (LSS) developed by Chelladurai and Saleh (1980), and a good leader can demonstrate all five types of behaviour. The LSS has forty items which measure the five types of behaviour and a number of studies have used this measure and found it to be valid and reliable.

Chelladurai states that there are three factors that affect leader behaviour:

- situational characteristics – for example, whether the opposition is weak or strong
- leader characteristics – such as experience, personality, etc.
- group member characteristics – including age, gender and experience of the members.

There are also three types of leader behaviour:

- required behaviour – what the situation requires the leader to do
- actual behaviour – what the leader actually does, which depends upon the above characteristics
- preferred behaviour – what the team members want the leader to do.

Figure 4.2 illustrates how all of these factors interact to affect performance.

According to this model it is important for leaders to be flexible depending upon the demands of each situation.

Commentary

Again, this model can go some way to explain how leader behaviour is developed and the effect that this can have on performance. However, there are also some criticisms of the model. The information again comes from self-report measures which could be seen to be subjective, although in this case they have been thoroughly tested. The majority of the research that has been carried out to test the theory has currently proved to be inconclusive.

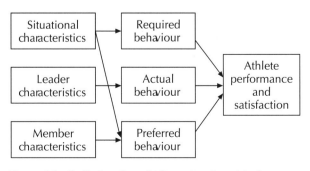

Figure 4.2: Chelladurai's multidimensional model of leadership

Successful leadership

Although there are a number of different styles of leadership, it is useful to examine which style leaders who are known to be successful use. RLA 18 illustrates the technique that Sir Alex Ferguson has used to lead Manchester United football team.

Real Life Application 18:

Sir Alex Ferguson

Sir Alex Ferguson

As manager of Manchester United Football Club, for fourteen years, Sir Alex Ferguson is probably one of the best known sports' leaders around. When he arrived in 1986, there were 30 people working full time for Manchester United and he got to know them all. Currently there are more than 400 staff and he knows many of them. Sir Alex is held in high regard by the staff due to a mixture of warmth and awed respect. It is clear that the majority of the players feel the same. He believes that the players are brought up to succeed which is fostered by the nurturing of young players at the club and through careful purchases of outsiders. Sir Alex believes that part of his success as a manager is due to time and control, control giving authority. He believes that players respect the fact that they know he will still be their manager tomorrow, thus enabling him to keep a careful control over his players.

Adapted from *FourFourTwo*, November 1999.

Summary

- Manchester United was the most successful football team in this country during the 1990s and Sir Alex Ferguson has been their manager throughout that time. Therefore he could be said to be one of the most successful managers of recent years.

Questions

1 What style of leadership do you believe that Sir Alex Ferguson adopts?

2 Why do you think it seems to work for Manchester United?

3 Explain his behaviour in terms of Chelladurai's five types of behaviour.

Player characteristics and leadership preference

There are a number of factors that can influence the leadership style preferences of sports players.

Age

Chelladurai and Carron (1983) carried out a study, using the LSS, with male basketball players. They found that younger players favoured a relationship-orientated approach, whilst the preference for an autocratic style of leadership actually increased linearly with age. Key Study 8 provides more detail about the relationship between leadership preference and age.

KEY STUDY 8

Researchers: Martin, Jackson, Richardson and Weiller (1999)

Aim: To investigate leadership style preference and age, comparing children's preferences with those of their parents.

Method: The LSS was given to 239 children and one of each of their parents. The children were aged between 10 and 18 and were taking part in a summer youth sports league.

Results: Both children and their parents wanted positive feedback from a leader and both wanted clear

---

instruction. Children, however, wanted to be allowed greater participation in decision making and scored significantly higher on the preference for a democratic leader. Children were also more concerned than their parents about a warm relationship with both the leader and the group, and wanted social support within the group.

Conclusions: This highlights that children and their parents do not always want the same characteristics from a coach or leader and therefore, just because the parent believes that their child would maximize his/her potential with a particular leader does not necessarily mean that the child will.

Gender

Although the research in this area is not totally conclusive, studies have found that women tend to prefer leaders to have a democratic style, whilst men slightly prefer leaders who show an autocratic style (Terry, 1984).

Horn and Glenn (1988) found that women who were high in competitive trait anxiety preferred coaches who provided support and positive feedback, whilst men's anxiety seems to be unrelated to preferred coaching style.

Ability level

Research has been mixed, however, Chelladurai and Carron (1983) found that skilled athletes preferred a more autocratic style of leadership.

Personality

Horn and Glenn (1988) found that athletes with an internal locus of control prefer coaches who excel in training and instructional behaviour, whilst those with an external locus of control prefer an autocratic leadership style.

Nationality

Chelladurai et al (1988) carried out a cross-cultural study looking at male Canadian and Japanese university athletes. They found that Japanese athletes preferred a more autocratic style of leadership and wanted more social support, whilst the Canadians preferred more training and instruction.

Commentary

Although some individual differences have been identified in leadership preference, it is important to remember that research into these factors has not been wholly conclusive. Some of the research studies have not been fully representative and therefore cannot be widely generalized. Thus the above differences should not be seen as 'concrete', rather they should provide 'food for thought'.

Therefore, for leaders to be successful there are a great number of factors that need to be taken into account. Often leaders may have many of the necessary characteristics but if the group that they are leading is not winning, the leader is considered to be unsuccessful (see RLA 19 for an example).

will be the best long-term option when replacing Keegan, regardless of whether he would be the fans first choice.

Adapted from *The Observer*, 8 October 2000, and *The Times*, 9 October 2000.

Summary

- Although Kevin Keegan was a very popular choice when he was appointed as England manager, his leadership skills appear not to have been very successful, as despite having some talented players in the team they failed to flourish under Keegan's management.

Real Life Application 19:

Kevin Keegan resigns

Kevin Keegan

Following the 1–0 defeat of the England football team in a World Cup qualifying match, the manager, Kevin Keegan resigned. He explained that he was resigning as he felt that he fell short of what was required in the job. Whilst he believed that he did lots of parts of the job adequately and some parts very well, he realized that he was inadequate at the key part of the job, getting the players to win matches. Keegan paid tribute to the players, whom had always been very supportive and put in the effort. As a manger, Kevin Keegan was honest, very popular with both the fans and the players, he was comfortable with the media interviews and passionate about football. It seems that his downfall was not having the tactical skills needed by a manager at international level.

There is a general belief now that the FA must have the courage to go for the man who they think

Questions

1 What was the main reason for Keegan resigning as England manager?

2 What types of leadership behaviour do you think that Keegan did show?

3 What type of leader would you have recommended that the FA appoint, bearing in mind the individual differences in leadership preference?

Essay questions

1 Aggression is an inevitable part of many sports. Discuss.

2 Describe how sporting performance may be affected by the presence of others.

3 Explain the importance of team and leader compatibility in sport.

# Advice on answering essay questions

When answering any question in connection with psychology and sport it is vitally important to remember to relate the psychological theory directly to sport, otherwise few marks will be awarded to your answers. Below are the main points that you should be including in the essay questions featured in this book, although these points are by no means exhaustive.

Chapter 1

1   Any theory from biological, humanistic, psychoanalytic or trait, although trait theory would probably be the most likely.

   Trait theorists (mention Eysenck and Cattell) propose that individuals have certain personality traits that are stable over time. Trait theories can be either single- or multi-trait and tend to be measured through self-report questionnaires. The theories suggest that some people have traits that make them more likely to participate in sport – for example, a competitive trait.

   The drawback with trait theories is that they do not take into account the effects of learning on individuals. Also, people do not behave in the same way in every situation and trait theory does not provide an explanation for this.

2   Firstly, describe the main features of operant conditioning, particularly the emphasis on reinforcement. The teacher could use the behaviour-shaping technique, praising the children each time they perform a forward roll that is nearly right and thus gradually moving the behaviour towards the required behaviour and praising the children when they have mastered the technique.

   Secondly, briefly explain what social learning theory is about, i.e. learning through imitation. The teacher could act as a model and demonstrate the forward roll, or s/he could show a video of a person carrying out a forward roll. The children would need to pay attention to this, remember what they had seen and put it into practice by trying to do forward rolls themselves.

3   Most likely suggestion would be the reciprocal style, however other styles are possible if justified. The footballers would work in pairs, following the teacher's instructions, taking it in turns to be the performer and the observer. They would give each other instant feedback and the teacher would monitor them closely. This style will work well as the footballers have the basic skills that they are now building upon.

Chapter 2

1   Allow children to pass through Veroff's three stages by not making sport too competitive for young children. It would be important to ensure that children do not lose intrinsic motivation as this would lead to an overall drop in motivation to take part (McClelland-Atkinson). Allow children to have repeated experiences of success to help develop levels of self-efficacy (Bandura) and feelings of personal competence (Harter).

2   Describe main theories: drive, inverted U, zone of optimal functioning, and catastrophe. Evaluate each linked to sport. Drive theory is too narrow due to the linear relationship. Inverted U allows for variations in arousal for different sports but the drawback is that if arousal goes beyond the optimal point performance is likely to suffer more than a steady decline. Zone of optimal functioning is good as it focuses on individual differences in arousal levels in sport, and catastrophe theory is appealing as it overcomes the problem of the inverted U theory.

3   Physiological measures are good due to their objectivity but may in themselves create feelings of anxiety. Self-report measures can be useful if they are strictly controlled but they depend upon the honesty of the participants and some people may misinterpret some questions. It is also difficult to remember how anxious you may have felt

retrospectively. Behavioural observation must have very strict criteria and be carried out by more than one observer. It is also questionable how easy it is to observe how anxious someone is feeling.

Chapter 3

1 Describe the four main types and when they should be used. A broad–external style is needed for taking in large amounts of information about the situation, and a broad–internal style is needed for examining self-information. A narrow–external style is needed for concentration, and a narrow–internal style is needed to focus on specific things. Examples from any sports should be added to highlight how all of these can be useful on different occasions.

2 Firstly, describe what imagery is linked specifically to sport. The uses of imagery include: enabling a sports player to focus, allowing practice whilst at home, and allowing practice without the pressure of being observed by others. As players imagine winning it is also likely to have a positive effect on self-confidence.

3 Define what is meant by an attributional retraining programme. The benefits for children would be that it could change the way that they see themselves and thus may alter their perceptions of their sporting ability. They would need to learn to attribute failure to factors such as lack of effort, and successes to ability, for the changes to occur.

Chapter 4

1 A distinction needs to be made between types of aggression and assertion, leading to an explanation of the inevitability of aggression. Also it would be useful to include detail of some of the factors that seem to link with aggression in sport. Techniques for reducing aggression would tie in well at the end.

2 Two types of influence are the audience and the co-action effect. Examine how performance may be affected and the factors that may lead to differences in sporting performance, referring to theories. Discussion of the notion of home-field advantage would be beneficial.

3 Describe the importance of team cohesion and what makes an effective leader. Factors that affect an individual's preference for leadership style should also be examined, leading to explanations about why compatibility between the leader and team is beneficial for sporting performance.

A Advice on answering short answer questions

Chapter 1

RLA 1

1 It raises the issue of whether the individuals were born with particular sporting ability or whether they learnt it by exposure to sport via other family members.

2 Born with certain traits that have remained stable over time that enable them to be successful in their particular field.

3 Sporting ability has been learnt by observing father/mother/sibling and copying their behaviour in an attempt to 'be like them'.

RLA 2

1 She won the heptathalon gold medal in Sydney 2000 and therefore has shown great ability over seven athletic events.

2 She has shown that she has great determination and vigour by the training programme she followed when she was younger and by the way she overcame injury. She did not give in and allow obstacles to prevent her achieving her aim.

RLA 3

1 UCS = karate class

  CS = karate suit

  UCR = anxiety

  CR = anxiety

2 Sam may develop a feeling of anxiety when he sees a type of white suit or white clothing, as his anxiety has been generalized onto similar stimuli.

3 Teach Sam to associate his karate suit with something pleasant – for example, wearing it to play with friends.

RLA 4

1 Wurz wore the boots once and won. Therefore wearing odd boots was reinforced (by winning) and according to the principles of operant conditioning a behaviour that is reinforced is likely to be repeated.

2 It allows them to focus their minds and they believe that if they complete the superstitious behaviours they will win, thus boosting their confidence.

RLA 5

1 Punishment.

2 Social learning theory.

3 By observing their heroes and seeing them get rewarded (status, money, etc.) children copy their behaviour and get rewarded vicariously.

RLA 6

1 Longer sessions would lead to children feeling tired, losing concentration and possibly starting to believe that they cannot be successful at that sport.

2 Repeated practice will hopefully lead to the children improving at a particular skill and thus this should improve their self-confidence and make them more willing to 'have a go' at other things.

3 It may lead children to attribute their behaviour incorrectly (see Chapter 3 for further details), leading to a lack of self-confidence and ultimately to a loss of interest in the sport.

Chapter 2

RLA 7

1 Intrinsically – he enjoyed taking part.

2 Intrinsic – enjoyment, playing with friends, etc.

  Extrinsic – praise from teacher, trophy for best team, etc.

3 The feedback is controlling (the captains are controlling his destiny) and informational (Jamie gets a negative message by being chosen at the end).

4 It will lead Jamie to feel that he does not have a sense of control over his participation and will make him feel that he is not personally competent by the fact everyone else was chosen before he was.

RLA 8

1 61.6%

2 The women's events are now seen as exciting to watch whereas they used to be seen as simply filling in time until the men's events.

3 It will make women more likely to approach an achievement situation.

RLA 9

1 Intrinsic levels reduced as he was not enjoying taking part.

Extrinsic levels reduced as the championship title could no longer be his.

2 The failure he had in Australia led to a temporary reduction in self-efficacy.

3 He had had repeated success in the past and therefore once he had overcome his doubts his self-efficacy was great enough to believe he could be successful again.

RLA 10

1 His arousal levels became so great that they actually led to an impairment of his performance.

2 He knew his arousal levels were too high and that if he did not attempt to control them it might lead to further reductions in performance.

3 A somatic technique for reducing arousal and anxiety.

Chapter 3

RLA 11

1 To see if there was any difference in performance between dissociative strategies that were connected to the sport and those that were neutral.

2 Coaches could teach all players how to use asso-ciative strategies more successfully rather than just the élite players.

RLA 12

1 No, an ability to switch between the styles would be most beneficial.

2 As it is a team game it is important that the team felt a sense of togetherness in their preparations (see Chapter 4 for more detail).

3 Internal imagery.

RLA 13

1 **a** Ability or task difficulty.

  b Effort.

2 Controllable unstable attributions.

3 Because they attributed their behaviour to factors that they had some control over and therefore would hopefully be able to change in the future to make them successful.

Chapter 4

RLA 14

1 They would say that the spectators became aggressive after watching the players become aggressive on the pitch, not letting the penalty be taken.

2 Frustration aggression would say that Celtic are frustrated because they are losing, and Rangers being awarded the penalty serves as a cue to release the aggression caused by their frustration.

3 Celtic being at home, losing during the game, the game being an important semi-final.

RLA 15

1 50%.

2 Home field advantage.

3 Factors include: familiarity with pitches, greater presence of fans, not having to travel, being acclimatized to the weather, media support.

RLA 16

1 All the players have a clearly identified position and each player knows they can depend upon the others to fulfil their roles, enabling every

player to concentrate on his particular role.

2 It is difficult to say whether success leads to cohesion or if cohesion leads to success.

3 A player of the same age and ability level as well as someone who is willing to take on a role and ensure that they put in as much effort as the existing team members.

RLA 17

1 Success.

2 Yes. Each member of the team is relying on the others performance and therefore, in order to succeed, they are all putting in maximum effort so that they will not let their team members down.

RLA 18

1 Autocratic in the main, although he does interact with the players in order to develop their skills.

2 Due to his success as a manager he has gained a high degree of respect which has led to players trusting his decisions. Players are also keen to experience the success that the team has had and thus will tend to accept his decisions.

3 • Instruction – clearly demonstrated by the teams success.

- Autocratic – demonstrated by the clear decision he makes about the players and the game plan.

- Democratic – discussion with the players as they are 'nurtured' at the club.

- Social support – again by knowing the staff and players so well he is able to support them when needed.

- Rewarding – both praise for players from Sir Alex after a good performance and success for the team when winning.

RLA 19

1 He felt that he was not successful enough at getting the team to win matches.

2 Social support for the players, positive reinforcement and some attempts at training and instruction.

3 A leader who uses quite an autocratic style, as this has been shown to be preferred both by men generally and by skilled sports players in particular, and therefore for a male international team this would be appropriate.

R Selected references

Chapter 1

Cattell, RB (1965). *The scientific analysis of personality*. Harmondsworth: Penguin.

Eysenck, H (1947). *Dimensions of personality*. London: Routledge and Kegan Paul.

Harlow, RG (1951). 'Masculine inadequacy and compensatory development of physique.' *Journal of personality*, 19, pp. 312–23.

Hollander, EP (1971). *Principles and methods of social psychology*. 2nd edn. New York: Oxford University Press.

Kroll, W and Crenshaw, W (1970). 'Multivariate personality profile analysis of four athletic groups.' In Cox, RH (1998) *Sport psychology – concepts and applications*. 4th edn. Iowa: WCB/McGraw-Hill.

Martens, R (1977). *Sport competition anxiety test*. Champaign, IL: Human Kinetics Publishers, Inc.

Moos, RH (1969). 'Sources of variance in responses to questionnaires and behaviour.' *Journal of abnormal psychology*, 74, pp. 405–12.

Morgan, WP (1979). 'Prediction of performance in athletics.' In Klavora, P and Daniel, JV (eds) *Coach, athlete, and the sport psychologist*. Champaign, IL: Human Kinetics Publishers.

Mosston, M and Ashworth, S (1986). *Teaching physical education*. Colombus, Ohio: Merrill Publishing Co.

Templin, DP and Vernacchia, RA (1995). 'The effect of highlight music videotapes upon the performance of intercollegiate basketball players.' *The sport psychologist*, 9, pp. 41–50.

Chapter 2

Anderson, MB and Williams, JM (1987). 'Gender role and sport competition anxiety: a re-examination.' *Research quarterly for exercise and sport*, 58, pp. 52–6.

Bandura, A (1977). 'Self-efficacy: toward a unifying theory of behavioural change.' *Psychological review*, 84, pp. 191–215.

Bond, MH (1986). *The psychology of Chinese people*. New York: Oxford University Press.

Burton, D (1988). 'Do anxious swimmers swim slower? Re-examining the elusive anxiety–performance relationship.' *Journal of sport and exercise psychology*, 10, pp. 45–61.

Deci, EL and Ryan, RM (1985). *Intrinsic motivation and self-determination in human behaviour*. New York: Plenum.

Doi, K (1985). 'The relation between the two dimensions of achievement motivation and personality of male university students.' *Japanese journal of psychology*, 56, pp. 107–10.

Duda, JL (1989). 'Relationship between task and ego orientation and the perceived purpose of sport among high school athletes.' *Journal of sport and exercise psychology*, 11, pp. 318–35.

Fazey, J and Hardy, L (1988). 'The inverted U hypothesis: a catastrophe for sport psychology?' *British Association of Sports Sciences monograph no. 1*, Leeds: The National Coaching Foundation.

Gill, DL and Deeter, TE (1988). 'Development of the SOQ.' *Research quarterly for exercise and sport*, 59, pp. 191–202.

Gould, D, Hodge, K, Peterson, K and Giannini, J, (1989). 'An exploratory examination of strategies used by élite coaches to enhance self-efficacy in athletes.' *Journal of sport and exercise psychology*, 11, pp. 128–40.

Gould, D, Petlichkoff, L and Weinberg, RS (1984). 'Antecedents of, temporal changes in, and relationships between CSAI-2 subcomponents.' *Journal of sport psychology*, 6, pp. 289–304.

Hanin, YL (1980). 'A study of anxiety in sport .' In Cox, RH (1998) *Sport psychology – concepts and applications*, 4th edn. Iowa: WCB/McGraw-Hill.

Harter, S (1978). 'Effective motivation reconsidered: towards a developmental model.' *Human development*, 21, pp. 34–64.

Harter, S (1982). 'The perceived competence scale for children.' *Child development*, 53, pp. 87–97.

Hull, CL (1951). *Essentials of behavior*. New Haven, CT: Yale University Press.

Jourden, FJ, Bandura, A and Banfield, JT (1991). 'The impact of conceptions of ability on self-regulatory factors and motor skill acquisition.' *Journal of sport and exercise psychology*, 13, pp. 213–26.

McClelland, DC, Atkinson JW, Clark RW, and Lowell EW (1953). *The achievement motive*. New York: Appleton-Century-Crofts.

Martens, R (1977). *Sport competition anxiety test.* Champaign, IL: Human Kinetics Publishers, Inc.

Martens, R and Landers, DM (1969). 'Motor performance under stress: a test of the inverted- U hypothesis.' *Journal of personality and social research,* 16, pp. 29–37.

Martens, R, Vealey, RS and Burton, D (1990). *Competitive anxiety in sport.* Champaign, IL: Human Kinetic Books.

Maslow, AH (1970). *Motivation and personality*. New York: Harper and Row.

Nelson, LL and Kagan, S (1972). 'Competition: the star-spangled scramble.' *Psychology Today,* 5, pp. 53–6.

Orlick, TD (1978). 'Winning through co-operation.' In Gill, D (1986) *Psychological dynamics of sport.* Champaign, IL: Human Kinetics Publishers Inc.

Oxendine, JB (1970). 'Emotional arousal and motor performance.' *Quest*, 13, pp. 23–30.

Page, SJ, Sime, W and Nordell, K (1999). 'The effects of imagery on female college swimmers perception of anxiety.' *The sport psychologist*, 13, pp. 458–69.

Sonstroem, RJ and Bernardo, P (1982). 'Intraindividual pre-game state anxiety and basketball performance: a re-examination of the inverted U curve.' *Journal of sport psychology*, 4, pp. 235–245.

Spence, KW (1956). 'Behavior theory and conditioning.' New Haven, CT: Yale University Press. In Cox, RH (1998) *Sports psychology – concepts and applications.* 4th edn. Iowa: WCB/McGraw-Hill.

Spielberger, CD (1971). 'Trait-state anxiety and motor behavior.' *Journal of motor behavior*, 3, pp. 265–79.

Vallerand, RJ and Losier, GF (1999). 'An integrative analysis of intrinsic and extrinsic motivators in sport.' *Journal of applied sport psychology*, vol. 11, no. 1, pp. 142–63.

Vallerand, RJ and Reid, G (1984). 'On the causal effects of perceived competence on intrinsic motivation: a test of cognitive evaluation theory.' *Journal of sport psychology*, 6, pp. 94–102.

Veroff, J (1969). 'Social comparison and the development of achievement motivation.' In Gill, DL (1986). *Psychological dynamics in sport*. Champaign IL: Human Kinetics Books.

Weinberg, RS and Hunt, UV (1976) 'The inter-relationship between anxiety, motor performance and electromyography.' *Journal of motor behavior,* 8, pp. 219–24.

Weinberg, RS and Jackson, A (1990). 'Building self-efficacy in tennis players: a coach's perspective.' *Journal of applied sport psychology*, 2, pp. 164–74.

Weiss, MR, and Horn, TS (1990). 'The relationship between children's accuracy and estimates of their physical competence and achievement-related characteristics.' *Research quarterly for exercise and sport*, 61, pp. 250–8.

Yerkes, RM and Dodson, JD (1908). 'The relationship of strength of stimulus to rapidity of habit formation.' *Journal of neurology and psychology,* 18, pp. 459–82.

Ziegler, SG (1978). 'An overview of anxiety management strategies in sport.' In Gill, DL (1986). *Psychological dynamics in sport*. Champaign IL: Human Kinetics Books.

Chapter 3

Bird, AM and Williams, JM (1980). 'A developmental-attributional analysis of sex-role stereotypes for sport performance.' *Developmental psychology*, 16 pp. 319–22.

Dweck, CS (1975). 'The role of expectations and attributions in the alleviation of learned helplessness.' *Journal of personality and social psychology*, 31, pp. 674–85.

Feltz, DL and Landers, DM (1983). 'The effects of mental practice on motor skill learning and performance: a meta-analysis.' *Journal of sport psychology,* 5, pp. 25–57.

Gill, DL and Strom, EH (1985). 'The effect of attentional focus on performance of an endurance task.' *International journal of sport psychology*, 16, pp. 217–23.

Hale, BD (1982). 'The effects of internal and external imagery on muscular and ocular concomitants.' *Journal of sport psychology*, 4, pp. 379–87.

Hall, CR, Rodgers, WM and Barr, KA (1990). 'The use of imagery by athletes in selected sports.' *The sports psychologist*, 4, pp. 1–10.

Hall, CR, Mack, D and Paivio, PC (1996). 'Imagery use by athletes: development of the Sport Imagery Questionnaire.' In Cox, RH (1998) *Sports psychology*

– concepts and applications. 4th edn. Iowa: WCB/McGraw- Hill.

Hanrahan, SJ, Grove, JR and Hattie, JA (1989). 'Development of a questionnaire measure of sport-related attributional style.' *International journal of sport psychology*, 20, pp. 114–34.

Heider, F (1944). 'Social perception and phenomenal causality.' *Psychological review,* 51, pp. 358–74.

Heider, F (1958). *The psychology of interpersonal relations*. New York: John Wiley and Sons.

McAuley, E, Duncan, TE and Russell, DW (1992). 'Measuring causal attributions: the revised causal dimension scale (CDSII).' *Personality and social psychology bulletin*, 18, pp. 566–73.

Mahoney, MJ and Avener, M (1977). 'Psychology of the élite athlete: an exploratory study.' *Cognitive therapy and behaviour research*, 1, pp. 135–41.

Masters, KS and Ogles, BM (1998). 'Associative and dissociative cognitive strategies in exercise and running: 20 years later, what do we know?' *The sport psychologist*, 12, pp. 253–70.

Moran, A (1993). 'Conceptual and methodological issues in the measurement of mental imagery skills in athletes.' *Journal of sport behavior*, 16, pp. 157–70.

Morgan, WP, O'Connor, PJ, Ellickson, KA and Bradley, PW (1988). 'Personality structure, mood states, and performance in élite male distance runners.' *International journal of sport psychology,* 19, pp. 247–63.

Morgan, WP and Pollock, ML (1977). 'Psychologic characterization of the élite distance runner.' In Cox, RH (1998) *Sports psychology – concepts and applications*. 4th edn. Iowa: WCB/McGraw- Hill.

Nideffer, RM (1976a). *The inner athlete: mind plus muscle for winning*. New York: Thomas Y Crowell Company.

Nideffer, RM (1976b). 'Test of attentional and interpersonal style.' *Journal of personality and social psychology,* 34, pp. 394–404.

Orbach, I, Singer, R and Price, S (1999). 'Attribution training program and achievement in sport.' *The sport psychologist*, 13 (1), pp. 69–82.

Pennebaker, JW and Lightner, JM (1980). 'Competition of internal and external information in an exercise setting.' *Journal of personality and social psychology*, 39, pp. 165–74.

Roberts, GC and Pascuzzi, D (1979). 'Causal attributions in sport: some theoretical implications.' *Journal of sport psychology*, 1, pp. 203–11.

Rodgers, W, Hall, C and Buckolz, E (1991). 'The effect of an imagery training program on imagery ability, imagery use and figure skating performance.' *Journal of applied sports psychology*, 3, pp. 109–25.

Rotter JB (1971). 'External control and internal control.' *Psychology today*, 5 (1), pp. 27–42, 58–9.

Russell, D (1982). 'The causal dimension scale: a measure of how individuals perceive causes.' *Journal of personality and social psychology*, 42, pp. 1137–45.

Scott, LM, Scott, D, Bedic, SP and Dowd, J (1999). 'The effect of associative and dissociative strategies on rowing ergometer performance.' *The sport psychologist*, 13 (1), pp. 57–68.

Van Schoyck, SR and Grasha, AF (1981). 'Attentional style variations and athletic ability: the advantages of the sports specific test.' *Journal of sport psychology*, 3, pp. 149–65.

Weiner, B (1972). *Theories of motivation: from mechanism to cognition*. Chicago: Rand McNally.

Chapter 4

Baron, R (1977). *Human aggression*. New York: Plenum Press.

Baron, R (1986). 'Distraction–conflict theory: progress and problems.' In Berkowitz, L (ed.) *Advances in experimental social psychology*, vol. 19, New York: Academic Press.

Berkowitz, L (1989). 'Frustration–aggression hypothesis: examination and reformulation.' *Psychological bulletin*, 106, pp. 59–73.

Berkowitz, L (1993). *Aggression: its causes, consequences and control*. Philadelphia: Temple University Press.

Bray, SR (1999). 'The home advantage from an individual team perspective.' *Journal of applied sport psychology,* vol. 11, no. 1, pp. 116–25.

Brunelle, JP, Janelle, CM and Tennant, LK (1999). 'Controlling competitive anger among male soccer players.' *Journal of applied sport psychology*, vol. 11, no. 2, pp. 283–97.

Chapman, AJ (1974). 'An electromyographic study of social facilitation: a test of the "mere presence" hypothesis.' *British journal of psychology*, 65, pp. 123–8.

Chelladurai, P (1984). 'Discrepancy between preferences and perceptions of leadership behaviour and satisfaction of athletes in varying sports.' *Journal of sport psychology*, 6, pp. 27–41.

Chelladurai, P (1990). 'Leadership in sports: a review.' *International journal of sport psychology*, 21, pp. 328–54.

Chelladurai, P and Carron, A (1983). 'Athletic maturity and preferred leadership.' *Journal of sport psychology*, 5, pp. 371–80.

Chelladurai, P and Saleh, SD (1980). 'Dimensions of leader behaviour in sports: development of a leadership scale.' *Journal of sport psychology*, 2, pp. 34–45.

Clayton, DA (1978). 'Socially facilitated behaviour.' *The quarterly review of biology*, 53, pp. 373–92.

Cottrell, NB (1968). 'Performance in the presence of other human beings: mere presence, audience, and affiliation effects.' In Simmell, EC, Hoppe, RA and Milton, GA (eds) *Social facilitation and imitative behavior*, Boston: Allyn and Bacon.

Courneya, KS and Carron, AV (1992). 'The home advantage in sport competitions: a literature review.' *Journal of sport and exercise psychology*, 14, pp. 13–27.

Earley, PC (1989). 'Social loafing and collectivism: A comparison of the United States and the People's Republic of China.' *Administrative science quarterly*, 34, pp. 565–81.

Fiedler, FE (1967). *A theory of leadership effectiveness*. New York: McGraw-Hill.

Goldstein, JH and Arms, RL (1971). 'Effects of observing athletic contests on hostility.' *Sociometry*, 34, pp. 83–90.

Ingham, AG, Levinger, G, Graves, J and Peckham, V (1974). 'The Ringelmann effect: studies of group size and group performance.' *Journal of experimental social psychology*, 10, pp. 371–84.

Kozub, SA and Button, C (2000). 'The influence of a competitive outcome on perceptions of cohesion in rugby and swimming teams.' *International journal of sport psychology*, 31, pp. 82–95.

Leonard, WM III (1989). 'The "home advantage": the case of the modern Olympics.' *Journal of sport behaviour*, 12, pp. 227–41.

Lewin, K, Lippitt, R and White, R (1939). 'Patterns of aggressive behaviour in experimentally created "social climates".' *Journal of social psychology*, 10, pp. 271–99.

Martens, R and Peterson, JA (1971). 'Group cohesiveness as a determinant of success and member satisfaction in team performance.' *International review of sport sociology*, 6, pp. 49–61.

Martin, SB, Jackson, AW, Richardson, PA and Weiller, KH (1999). 'Coaching preferences of adolescent youths and their parents.' *Journal of applied sport psychology,* vol. 11, no. 2, pp. 247–62.

Pollard, R (1986). 'Home advantage in soccer: a retrospective analysis.' *Journal of sport sciences,* 4, pp. 237–48.

Reifman, AS, Larrick, RP and Fein, S (1991). 'Temper and temperature on the diamond: the heat aggression relationship in major league baseball.' *Personality and social psychology bulletin*, 17, pp. 580–5.

Russell, GW (1974). 'Machiavellianism, locus of control, aggression, performance and precautionary behaviour in ice hockey.' *Human relations*, 27, pp. 825–37.

Russell, GW (1981). 'Spectator moods at an aggressive sporting event.' *Journal of sport psychology*, 3, pp. 217–27.

Russell, GW and Drewery, BR (1970). 'Crowd size and competitive aspects of aggression in ice hockey.' *Human relations,* 29, pp. 723–35.

Schwartz, B and Barsky, SF (1977). 'The home advantage.' *Social forces,* 55, pp. 641–61.

Silva, JM (1979). 'Behavioural and situational factors affecting concentration and skill performance.' *Journal of sport psychology*, 1, pp. 221–7.

Steiner, ID (1972). *Group processes and productivity*. New York: Academic Press.

Triplett, N (1898). 'The dynamogenic factors in pacemaking and competition.' *American journal of psychology*, 9, pp. 507–53.

Tuckman, BW (1965). 'Developmental sequences in small groups.' *Psychological bulletin*, 63, pp. 384–99.

Varca, PE (1980). 'An analysis of home and away game performance of male college basketball teams.' *Journal of sport psychology*, 3, pp. 245–57.

Wann, DL (1997). *Sport psychology*. New Jersey: Prentice Hall.

Widmeyer, WN, Brawley, LR, and Carron, AV (1990). 'The effects of group size in sport.' *Journal of sport and exercise psychology*, 12, pp. 177–90.

Zajonc, RB (1965). 'Social facilitation.' *Science*, 149, pp. 269–74.

Zillman, D, Johnson, RC and Day, KD (1974). 'Provoked and unprovoked aggression in athletes.' *Journal of research in personality*, 8, pp. 139–52.

Index